Praise for
Positive Infusion

"In *Positive Infusion*, Victoria Winters shows you how to notice the choices you make and to align them with your heart's desires. Her message is simple, powerful and transformational."
 —CHRISTINE LEE, International best-selling author of, *My Hero*

"We've heard that you can do anything you want to do. Getting out of your own way helps. This book tells you the easiest ways to take yourself anywhere you want to go in life. What a delightful, fun and pleasure ride to all out joy."
 —M. SHAWN PETERSEN, author of *Stella and the Time Keepers*

"In the years that I have known the author Victoria Winters, I have never heard an unkind word, a "poor me", a whine, or anything other than a positive attitude, an audible smile and solutions rather than problems. Victoria is the master of positivity and joyful living, so it only makes sense that her latest book *Positive Infusion* would be dedicated to teaching us the secrets that she uses to guide her own life."
 —DAN STREECH, President, Nordhaven Yachts

"Like a day at the spa, I feel calmer, more relaxed and ready to step into my own greatness. Everyone can use a *Positive Infusion*. A must read!"
 —SABRINA NORMAN, author of *From Having a Boss to Being The Boss*

"*Positive Infusion* is something we need just as the air that we breathe."
 —PEGGY MCCOLL, New York Times Best Selling Author

"Find a way to get everyone in your sphere of influence to read *Positive Infusion—Master the Choice to Feel Good!* There's nothing better than feeling great and being surrounded by other people who choose to go for the best in life."
—**Cheryl Barnes Cabasso**, Singer

"Wow, I've got goosebumps from my first read of *Positive Infusion*. What a breath of fresh air filled with positive change, uplifting ideas, amazing stories, and exercises that will stretch your imagination if you choose to apply the incredible suggestions. I love how the author awakens the self-appreciation aspect in each of us. This book is bursting with love!

Positive Infusion is a must-read, so grab your copy now and discover the magnificent person you really are. Absolute must read!"
—**Vladimira Kuna**, International best-selling author of *The Bible of The Masterminds*

POSITIVE INFUSION

POSITIVE INFUSION

VICTORIA WINTERS

Copyright © 2022 by Victoria Winters
All rights reserved. No part of this publication may be reproduced, stored in a retrieval system or transmitted in any form or by any means, electronic, mechanical, photocopying or otherwise, without the prior written permission of the copyright owner. Permissions should be addressed in writing to the author. Contact the author: support@VictoriaWintersAuthor.com

Disclaimer:
This book is written to provide information, motivation and enjoyment to its readers. It is sold with the understanding that the author and publisher are not providing any type of psychological, legal, or other kind of professional advice. The content of the book is the sole expression and opinion of its author. No warranties or guarantees are expressed or implied by the author and the publisher's choice to include any of the content in this volume. Neither the publisher nor the author shall be liable for any physical, psychological, emotional, financial, or commercial damages, including, but not limited to special, incidental, consequential or other damages. Our views and rights are the same: Each is responsible for their own choices, actions and results.

Published by:
Caravelle Associates Publishing
Lance Buckley, cover design
David Moratto, interior design

First Edition.
Printed in the United States of America.

Library of Congress Control Number: 2021908299

Publisher's Cataloging-In-Publication Data

Names: Winters, Victoria, author.
| McColl, Peggy, 1958- writer of supplementary textual content.
Title: Positive infusion / Victoria Winters ; [foreword by Peggy McColl].
Description: First edition. | [Laguna Beach, California] : Caravelle Associates Publishing, [2021] | Includes bibliographical references.
Identifiers: ISBN 9780578849522 (trade paperback) | ISBN 9780578903118 (ebook)
Subjects: LCSH: Choice (Psychology) | Attitude (Psychology) | Positive psychology. | Happiness.
Classification: LCC BF611 .W56 2021 (print) | LCC BF611 (ebook) | DDC 153.83--dc23

Lovingly dedicated

*To Evelyn V.
… miraculous beginning*

&

*To Crystal V.
… glorious continuing*

CONTENTS

FOREWORD BY PEGGY MCCOLL . . . . *xi*
INTRODUCTION . . . . *xiii*

part one
WORTHINESS

1. YOU ARE WORTHY OF EVERYTHING YOU DESIRE *3*
2. BUILD YOUR SELF-ESTEEM – ASK THOUGHT-PROVOKING QUESTIONS *13*
3. LOVE AND ORIGINALITY – THE MAGNIFICENT YOU *21*

part two
CLARITY

4. TO BE – FREEDOM AND OTHER MIRACULOUS IDEAS *43*
5. CLARIFY YOUR DESIRE – ASK AND EXPECT AN ANSWER *59*
6. MASTER THE CHOICE TO FEEL GOOD *67*

part three
AFFIRMATION

7. ABSOLUTE POWER – APPLY MAGNUM FORCE *81*
8. ONE QUESTION A DAY – AN AFFIRMATION IN PLAY *93*
9. GOOD – THE ONLY REALITY OF BEING *101*

APPENDIX *109*
ACKNOWLEDGEMENTS *111*
RESOURCES *117*
ABOUT THE AUTHOR *123*

FOREWORD BY PEGGY MCCOLL

I WAS BLESSED TO meet Victoria Winters, the author of *Positive Infusion* a number of years ago when I was invited to speak at an event in Los Angeles. The moment I saw her, I could feel positive energy exuding from her. She had a wonderful presence and after getting to know her over the years, and after reading her book, it is obvious that she has a deep understanding for how to live a fulfilling life.

Positive Infusion is a delightful book that can inspire you to look at your life as the gift that it is. When I began my journey into self-discovery back in January 1979, books that offered simple understanding for how to create success, such as *Positive Infusion,* were not available. Yes, there were self-help books available at that time, but none explained, in laymen's terms, the way to success. This inspired me to write my first book, and here I am today, nineteen books later, and feeling blessed to serve the world in positive ways. Another blessing in my life is the work that I do with authors, as I guide them to help others. Victoria Winters is a graduate from my Complete Author Program, and she created one of the most enjoyable books that I have read from any of my graduates.

The truth is that if you want your life to change for the better, *you* must change for the better. With discipline and great guidance, you can certainly begin at once to create positive change in your life.

Victoria has provided you with a gold mine of valuable content inside these pages, and it would serve you well to study this book and implement her recommendations. Perhaps you want to create a study group for *Positive Infusion* and discuss the many ways to implement these strategies and experience wonderful new results in your life.

My wish for you is only success. Have fun in the study of *Positive Infusion* and may you be blessed with an abundance of the things you desire.

—Peggy McColl, *New York Times* Best-Selling Author

INTRODUCTION

THINKING POSITIVE THOUGHTS is good advice. It is easy enough to do if you believe it. You naturally feel good when you are doing things you love and enjoy. The situations and circumstances you find yourself enjoying feel effortless while time seems to dissolve into an atmosphere of pure joy. It's easy to feel good, and yet it is even easier to move yourself in the opposite direction. Have you ever wondered about negativity and why you would ever choose to move away from positive joy? In a word, the answer is simply *habit*.

A habit is a tendency to perform a certain action or behave automatically in a particular manner. It is formed by doing something often—until it requires no conscious effort or the need to make a decision in the moment. In other words, a set of actions can become automatic. The ability to form a habit can serve you well because it frees you to direct your attention toward something you consciously choose to do automatically.

A habit gets stronger through repetition of actions. Practicing doing something repeatedly, over time, will solidify any action into a set pattern that can be recalled automatically on your behalf. It's nice to know that you have the power to create an automatic program that will save you time and effort.

You have the ability to change any habit that does not serve your ideal purpose. You probably have established habits that you are unaware of that counteract moving your fondest dreams into physical reality. Changing a habit is not easily accomplished. This is a good thing, because habits serve you, and you can create a new habit any time you want. Therefore, you do not have to fight with yourself to change a habit. Simply form a new one.

Forming a new habit is easy. All that is required is to perform an action repeatedly over a period of time. Understand that your existing habits are based upon beliefs held in your mind. And just like the habit, a belief will cause you to do things a certain way. Likewise, you can change any belief by replacing it with a new one based upon new information you discern as true.

You are a magnificent human being and you hold the cards for your success. Whatever you want to achieve, experience, or do is entirely up to you. Perhaps you do not believe you are actually the only person in control of your life. Here is how you can easily prove it to yourself. Ask yourself questions and honestly answer them.

The ancient Greek philosopher, Socrates, never lectured students. He taught primarily by asking questions. In fact, he never committed anything to writing. I am unaware of another author of the time who wrote specifically about Socretes' teaching method. However, Plato was his student and many scholars point out the differences between the two philosophers' points of view. Socrates' challenged conventional wisdom of the day. Knowing how to ask questions epitomizes the meaningfulness of Socrates's perhaps best implied philosophy, *"The unexamined life is not worth living."* Another way to understand the statement would be to realize that living life without discovering what you want, what you dream of, would become an intolerable existence. *"True wisdom comes to each of us when we realize how little we understand about life, ourselves and the world around us."*—SOCRATES

The purpose of a question is to seek a solution to a problem. In this instance, the problem is to understand the way you control your own life. Now, equipped with the solution, use it to your advantage. Decide to form a new, positive habit or pattern. Decide to set it and forget it so it works for you automatically.

It is vitally important to focus on the positive. Even in the midst of negativity, you can become more positive about enjoying the life you rightly deserve. And even if you currently believe that some of your thoughts are great for other people, but you feel those thoughts cannot be your personal experience, think again. Whatever you have in your mind belongs exclusively to you and with a new habit working for you, you can manifest something you would love into your personal reality.

It does not matter where you live, the number of years you have lived so far, what you look like or what you have done up until now. You have the ability and opportunity to think positively and to proceed directly toward whatever you want.

Once upon a time, I wanted a new car. And not just any car. I wanted a Mercedes Benz. I owned a car that provided adequate transportation. All automobiles are designed to get the driver from point A to B, but the style of motoring along is a choice. Let's face it, some cars are magnificent and I happen to think of a Mercedes as my dream car.

I believed that because of my job (or lack thereof) I could not afford to purchase a luxury car, at least not in my foreseeable future. But I still felt a burning desire to drive a nicer vehicle and specifically that brand of automobile. This idea popped up every time I drove up to an establishment that offered valet parking. I preferred self-parking because I felt my current car was simply not worthy of me. My car had become aesthetically unpleasing.

One day I accepted an invitation to join a girlfriend for lunch at a very fashionable restaurant. I had not seen her for many years, but I knew her to be a socially conscious status seeker and exceptionally financially successful. I planned to dress elegantly and arrive early to find an inconspicuous parking place. As I drove to the restaurant, I listened to marvelous music which enhanced my mood along the way. I felt like a million bucks. I could hardly wait to see her and enjoy the luncheon.

Arriving at the restaurant, to my surprise, valet parking appeared to be the only available parking option. Although not in my plans, I decided to deal with retrieving my car later. How difficult could it be to simply call for my car after my friend retrieved hers? Problem solved.

Lunch was amazing and I thoroughly enjoyed our visit. The time came to head home, and then I remembered my car. I wanted to exit the scene gracefully and imagined my friend getting into her vehicle and driving away ahead of me. Walking together toward the exit, I told her how much I enjoyed our time together and hoped to see her again soon. I chose to delay going to the valet booth, so I politely excused myself to the woman's room and bid her farewell. I felt this was my best course of action. I wanted to keep my friend from seeing my embarrassing car.

A few minutes later I made my way to the valet booth to claim my car. To my surprise a large crowd of people had formed and they were all waiting for their cars. I noticed my friend standing in the group and she waved for me to join her. Stepping toward her I glanced at cars coming forward and watched some people in the crowd retrieving their automobiles. I thought my friend would have been motoring on her way by now and I could simply exit anonymously. Unease washed over me and I again experienced the previous uncomfortable feeling of being forced to use valet parking. My friend looked so happy, poised and confident. While I stood there contemplating my discomfort, her car arrived. Just as I thought, it was a late model luxury car. We hugged, said our goodbyes, and she proceeded down the stairs to her car.

Breathing a sigh of relief, I thought my plan had worked out after all. She could drive away ahead of me without catching a glimpse of my vehicle. This is what I hoped for; however I continued to feel uneasy. In the next moment another car pulled up behind my friend's car, and I could see her standing adjacent to the open door of her car. I thought to myself: *If she would just get inside and drive off now, I still have a chance to keep my car anonymous and exit sight unseen.* Suddenly, I heard the voice of a valet loudly shout: "Who's car is this?"

The valet's announcement sliced through me like a stiff wind and I suddenly felt hot and momentarily unable to move. As he vigorously waived his hand while searching the crowd for the owner, I could feel the blood rising to my face. He had announced my car!

Up to this point no valet had made a similar declaration. I felt mortified. The crowd of people waiting had only slightly dissipated, and it was impossible for me to easily descend the stairs without calling attention to myself. I looked around to see if my friend had driven away. Naturally, she was still there. My shoes felt like cement bricks as I took one laborious step after another descending the steps toward my car. The valet's resounding question triggered a response. Everyone in the crowd looked around for the car's owner.

In a flash, all eyes in the awaiting crowd turned toward me like a school of fish suddenly changing direction simultaneously. I was exposed as the owner of the ugliest car in the world. If it's possible to turn shades of red and purple—like a chameleon changes shades of green—I thought I had done so.

Could my obsession with an idea I did not want to experience have caused this drama to play out in this iniquitous fashion? The very thing I had dreaded started to run like a well-rehearsed play. Reaching my car, I quietly handed the valet my ticket and a small tip. Buckling the seat belt as fast as possible, I lowered my eyes and drove to the nearest exit staring straight ahead to avoid eye contact with my friend, the crowd and the other drivers.

Several days following my imagined humiliation, I decided to do something about improving my transportation. I had no idea how I would obtain the money to buy my dream car, but I decided it was not worth spending time lamenting over something as unpleasant as working harder or getting a second job just to buy a car. Remembering those humiliating feelings became a shield guarding my mind from any related thoughts that could ruin my good mood. One of the things I like about myself is my propensity and determination to feel good most of the time.

Of late I had been working with a headhunter to find a new job. One day I got a call for an interview. Happily, I drove to the company and imagined rolling along in my new Mercedes. In an effort to feel better about my current situation, I decided to have some fun whenever taking a drive. I would clearly visualize the star emblem on the hood of my car. Travelling along scenic routes and even passing through city centers that mostly escaped my gaze, I felt wrapped in a smooth leather seat that cushioned every bump on the road. As I controlled the wheel of my magnificent car, time seemed to evaporate and I arrived at my destination more quickly than seemed possible. I loved what I called, *sessions with my dream car*. This became a fun game to play with myself because it helped me relax and enjoy driving.

My interview went well and I expected to be offered a position. True to my expectation, the headhunter called me with an offer of employment that included a sign on bonus. If I agreed to stay with the company for one year, they were prepared to offer me a lump sum to accept the job. Up to this point in my career I had never received a bonus to accept employment and especially not for the amount of money this company proposed. Short story shorter, I purchased my Mercedes Benz with the bonus money.

It is wonderful to think about things you would love to experience. This thinking positively breathes life into your dreams. Positive thinking will infuse your mind with love, joy, happiness and cause you to experience things in your physical reality that precisely harmonize with your most ardent thoughts and feelings. The most invigorating thing to keep in mind is you need not have any idea or concept of how to cause the manifestation of your wildest dreams. And that's the fun part because it is not your job or duty to know *how*. You must become proficient in thinking positively. In other words, think about things that cause you to feel good. And this you can do though repetition of doing things according to your own ideas. In simple terms, develop new habits.

Cultivating a new habit does not make the old habit disappear immediately. In fact, you'll experience a mighty push back from your old habit to keep you doing the same things. Remember, a habit is strong and will oppose being replaced. This is fantastic when the habit is in tune with your desire for the good you deserve.

It will take effort on your part to think more positively, but the rewards for making the effort are astonishing. Quickly, you will begin to notice changes in your feelings and results when you start focusing on things you want while denying the excuses and words that tell you to give up. One way to calm the flooding negative self-talk is to ask yourself questions. In the midst of negative thoughts seeking to hold you in place, pause and ask this question: "What am I thinking about?" The practice of switching your thoughts to something that feels better can be established as an automatic thing. If you want to instantly see something better unfold in your personal reality, pay attention more often to how you feel and what you are thinking about. All that is required is to ask and honestly answer questions you pose to yourself. Find out what's really going on inside of you.

I've written this book in part to share some personal experiences that have helped me to live life more abundantly and on purpose. I also want to offer ideas that may help you to live the life you want to enjoy on your terms. This book is designed to help you ask yourself questions to examine your beliefs. It will also help you better understand yourself and how you must get out of your own way and allow prosperity to easily come to you.

Getting to know yourself better is a powerful way to take control of your life. Give up blame, worry, sorrow, struggle and anything that opposes feeling good. Your life is yours for the enjoyment of living and experiencing happiness and love. Nothing matters more than feeling good and you can do this when you decide to pay greater attention to the way you feel and act accordingly.

I'm still learning and applying things I learn. This is a lifelong practice that will keep you fascinated and fully engaged in the livingness of your own life experiences. In British English the word *livingness* means, "the condition or quality of having life and being alive." No one beside you can decide and implement how you think and conduct your life. If nothing else, understand that no other person can live your life for you. Learn to care more about how you feel. The journey to paying attention to what you think versus being concerned about what others may think is your real work. Life is a glorious ride and especially so when you become captain of the freeway!

Spirit is life and it is within you to expand and express the livingness of your life. To live your life in ways that are pleasing to you is the ultimate purpose of life. And as a result, you help other people along the way. For what other purpose would you propose other than increasing expansion and expression of pure joy?

part one
WORTHINESS

chapter one

YOU ARE WORTHY OF EVERYTHING YOU DESIRE

"Desire is the effort of the unexpressed possibility within, seeking expression without, through your action."
—Wallace Wattles

THE WAY YOU feel about yourself is everything. Whatever you desire—to do, to go or to acquire—is within your realm of possibility. Have you ever wondered why you want a particular thing? Most likely you are seeking more love, comfort, ease and happiness. After all, increasing any good thing simply feels better.

Going to work for an employer is one idea many people accept as a means to an end. Earning money to maintain a lifestyle sounds easy enough to accomplish. Get a job, go to work, pay your bills and enjoy yourself with whatever is left over from your earnings. This approach appears to be an established order of operation for society. Of course, if you want more than a mediocre lifestyle, you may search for opportunities to increase your happiness by engaging in various personal, social and recreational activities. Moreover, take a fabulous vacation from mundane routines as often as possible.

As the patterns of habitual behavior play out in situations and circumstances you observe, there will be moments when you question why you ever do something that you do not enjoy. The familiar clichés which remind us to take control of life and pursue our dreams are too often ignored.

Before we had the internet, books, magazines, brochures and

travel agents were my primary sources of research about places to visit. A visit to San Francisco had been on my mind. At this juncture, spending time reading, day dreaming and imagining myself doing things outside of my regular routine became my greatest activity for vicarious adventures. Fresh out of college and living on my own afforded me the invincible peace of mind shared among many young people in search of freedom, romance and purpose.

Planning a trip can be as much fun as inhabiting the physical location. My propensity for living the "good life" often upset the precarious balance between my dreams and current financial status. However, seeing and feeling the experiences in my imagination persisted, so I quietly ignored the fact that my cash fell short for fulfilling the plans. Instead of dwelling on a temporary reality that could potentially thwart my dream, I told myself that I could always change the length of my stay to accommodate the breadth of my dollars.

The Mark Hopkins is a luxury hotel located at the top of Nob Hill in San Francisco, California. Opened in 1926, the location previously accommodated a mansion built by the hotel's namesake as a dream home for his wife. The mansion's construction was completed in 1878 after the death of Mark Hopkins. His wife, Mary Sherwood Hopkins, bequeathed the Nob Hill mansion to her second husband, Edward Francis Searles. In 1893, Searles donated the grounds and building to the San Francisco Art Association for use as a school and museum. Surviving the 1906 San Francisco earthquake, the mansion later succumbed to the three-day fire that followed the great quake.

A mining engineer and hotel investor, George D. Smith, purchased the Nob Hill site, removed the Art Association building and began construction of a luxurious hotel. One of the most distinguishing features about the Nob Hill location is the magnificent view. The nineteen-story hotel, a combination of French chateau and Spanish ornamentation, is home to the famous Top of the Mark lounge.

A dreamer loves a superb view if for no other reason than to expand upon their visions while physically standing on higher ground. With determination, vision and sticking to my plan, I spent three glorious days surrounded in elegance and luxury at the Mark Hopkins Hotel. I know you rightly deserve everything you desire because you are the dreamer in your own life.

If—by Rudyard Kipling
If you can keep your head when all about you
Are losing theirs and blaming it on you,
If you can trust yourself when all men doubt you,
But make allowance for their doubting too;
If you can wait and not be tired by waiting,
Or being lied about, don't deal in lies,
Or being hated, don't give way to hating,
And yet don't look too good, nor talk too wise:

If you can dream—and not make dreams your master;
If you can think—and not make thoughts your aim;
If you can meet with Triumph and Disaster
And treat those two impostors just the same;
If you can bear to hear the truth you've spoken
Twisted by knaves to make a trap for fools,
Or watch the things you gave your life to, broken,
And stoop and build 'em up with worn-out tools:

If you can make one heap of all your winnings
And risk it on one turn of pitch-and-toss,
And lose, and start again at your beginnings
And never breathe a word about your loss;
If you can force your heart and nerve and sinew
To serve your turn long after they are gone,
And so hold on when there is nothing in you
Except the Will which says to them: 'Hold on!'

> If you can talk with crowds and keep your virtue,
> Or walk with Kings—nor lose the common touch,
> If neither foes nor loving friends can hurt you,
> If all men count with you, but none too much;
> If you can fill the unforgiving minute
> With sixty seconds' worth of distance run,
> Yours is the Earth and everything that's in it,
> And—which is more—you'll be a Man, my son!

Kipling's poem presents a series of suggestions that come down to very simple advice. If you have the courage to follow your ideas, you will enjoy yourself and live the life of your dreams.

WHAT IS YOUR REASON FOR DENYING YOURSELF ANYTHING YOU REALLY WANT?

There is an answer for every question. Be mindful and take care. A list of excuses for avoiding pursuing your dreams is *not* the best answer to the question. Your answer to this question contains a solution you can use to your advantage.

Human beings are incredible. You are fabulousness walking around. You help other people on a regular basis. Your presence here on earth is a necessary part of the continuous experiences everyone gets to enjoy. You make it possible for other people to enjoy their lives. You are worthy of everything you desire. Consequently, not everything you focus upon is worthy of you.

Speak empowering words and notice how you feel. Deep within your soul you connect with the truth about yourself and your life. Nothing outside of you can link to your feelings about your life in such a personal manner. This is true because your feelings are inside you. They are your personal and unique connection to all that life *is*.

The way you see yourself is also how other people see you. You can test this statement in physical practice even without speaking words. Your feelings operate much the same as radio waves. Both are invisible to the eye, yet both can be tuned to any particular frequency or channel. Feelings and radio waves can be physically experienced as movement within your physical body. Notice how easily you use your power to change to a different frequency. Think of a song you love. Now imagine yourself sitting on a colorful towel on a sandy beach. The inner workings of your power to choose something you want to observe causes a change of feeling almost instantly.

One unique feature about your feelings is the precise service they render. Think of your feelings as your very own personal guidance system. Feelings directly deliver information and tell you precisely where you stand in relation to your desire. As you pay attention to the way you feel while holding yourself in high esteem, you will notice the instant you deviate from proceeding in the direction you want to go. In other words, your movement toward the thing you really want resides in a place accessible on the path that leads directly to it. If you turn away from it, you will immediately notice a change in how you feel because you are moving away from your desire; quite literally; you are travelling in the opposite direction.

A change in direction is often as subtle as a gnat landing on a leaf. To think one thought contrary to what you want is the same as going toward something you do not want. Imagine a staircase. Take a step up and then a step down. Although you may feel as if you are in the same place, you have actually moved forward to a new place and changed direction to occupy a different place, albeit, a familiar one.

We live in a world of motion, and everything is in a constant state of movement. Because you can control your actions, you are better served by training yourself to think more often about something you want. Physics tells us that no two objects can occupy the same space. The place your object of desire occupies stands ready for you to claim it. And whether you can see it with your physical eyes or not, it is real and you can move directly to it by taking the path that leads to where it currently resides.

The good news about everything being in a constant state of motion is this: The thing you want is also moving. It is either moving toward you or away from you. The movement toward you happens as a result of the intensity of your feelings and thoughts about the thing you want. This is true because of natural, universal laws which govern the universe. You have the power to cause the thing you want to come to you easily just as you have the power to push it away.

Every human being has the ability to manifest thoughts into physical form. Therefore, every human being is powerful. The difference between individuals may be found in the operational function rather than the ability. To fine tune a skill requires practice and willingness to improve the quality of a skill being performed.

When you entertain an idea about something you would love to experience in physical reality, that idea is yours immediately. You own it just the same as if you paid for it with cash and brought it home. The same is true of ideas you do not want to experience in physical or mental reality.

HOW MUCH ATTENTION DO YOU PAY TO THINGS THAT YOU DO NOT WANT?

Esteem means to value, to have great regard for and to hold a favorable opinion of something. The word self-esteem solidifies the necessity to understand the importance of cultivating better and better opinions of yourself and others.

"Don't compromise yourself, you are all you've got."—JANIS JOPLIN, AMERICAN SONGWRITER (1943–1970).

To observe and to contemplate anything other than the good you desire and rightly deserve is to separate yourself from a part of *you*. Believe it or not, your opinion about you is the only one that really matters to you. How would you describe yourself to another person?

EXERCISE:
1. Write a description of yourself in abundant detail. Use words that describe the real you according to your present vision of yourself.
2. Read the words you have written out loud and pay careful attention to every word.
3. Notice how you feel. If you feel the slightest sensation of anything unpleasant, look at the word that triggered the feeling.
4. Are the words in your description your honest opinion or the opinion of another person?
5. If you have adopted any words from the opinions of another person that feel unpleasant, why would you use those words?

Language is an expression of thought and feeling. Recognizing your life's purpose and being fully aware of your choices increases your capacity to become the person you desire. All things will be expressed in your daily activities.

Young children many times display what they think about themselves at any given moment. Their games of dress up and pretending to be another character reveals the truth about the person they'd love to be. Far beyond childhood pretense, adults engage in the same process; however they may be inhibited by previously programed ideas that dictate the boundaries of acceptable adult behavior.

Where did the idea come from that the image you hold of yourself shall be defined for you by outside standards you may or may not agree with? Shall you believe you must act according to any image presented to you by someone else as if it is a standard for your compliance? The way you feel and see yourself has a lot to do with things you will choose for yourself.

The image you hold of yourself is the best place to begin to understand your power to control the experiences you want to enjoy. To say this is an "inside job" pales in relation to understanding your true nature. You are magnificent!

Asking yourself questions and examining the answers will reveal a deeper understanding of the power you possess to live life on your terms. You may also discover, quite unexpectedly, the ways you have been keeping yourself from doing things you really want to do. Hold yourself in higher self-esteem and understand the reason you must pay attention to your feelings. Decide to choose better thoughts. This practice will open the doors you may now think of as unavailable or closed.

Words are powerful. The sequence and frequency in which a pattern of thought, (words arranged in a particular order), travel through your mind ignite feelings within. To feel happy or sad by choice is within your capacity. You can allow your attention to flow in either direction.

The characterization of three wise monkeys, Mizaru, who sees not, Kikazaru, who hears not and Iwazaru, who speaks not, is a funny and excellent image to recall. A seventeenth century carving of the three wise monkeys is over a door of the famous Tosho-gu shrine in Nikko, Japan. In Chinese, a similar phrase, "Look not at what is contrary to propriety; listen not to what is contrary to propriety; speak not what is contrary to propriety; make no movement which is contrary to propriety," epitomizes the famous monkey images and finds the origin of their words in the late Analects of Confucius from the second to the fourth century B.C.

Simple messages that amuse and spark your sense of humor are excellent. You simply cannot get it wrong because everything you feel and act upon is entirely up to you.

"As long as you allow things to seem real to you, you are putting your energy into it. You are nurturing it; you are feeding it; you are keeping it alive; you are putting your faith into that thing, whether you like it or not, and it must naturally grow for the law of growth is ever working to produce whatever seed you plant."—RAYMOND HOLLIWELL

chapter two

BUILD YOUR SELF-ESTEEM—ASK THOUGHT-PROVOKING QUESTIONS

Day 1

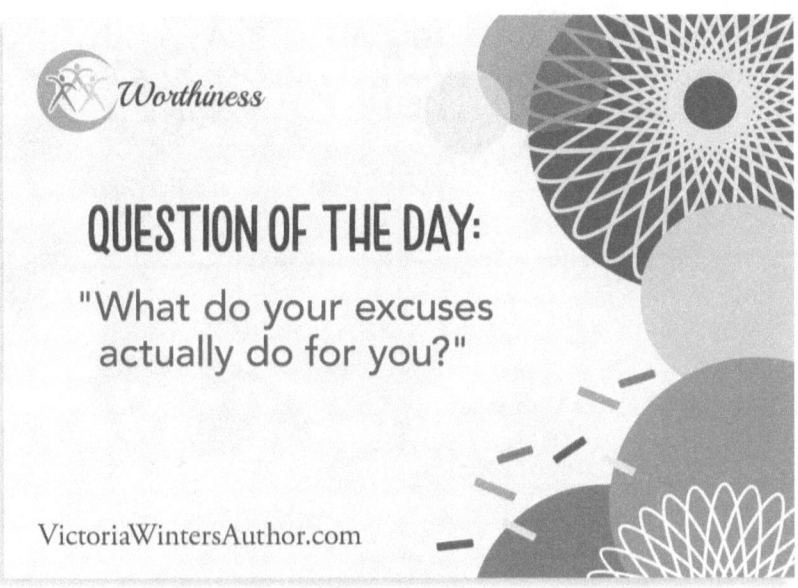

"For some strange reason, we tend to minimize the goals that we can accomplish. And for some equally strange reason, we think other people can do things that we cannot. You must understand that you have deep reservoirs of talent and ability within you."

—EARL NIGHTINGALE

Day 2

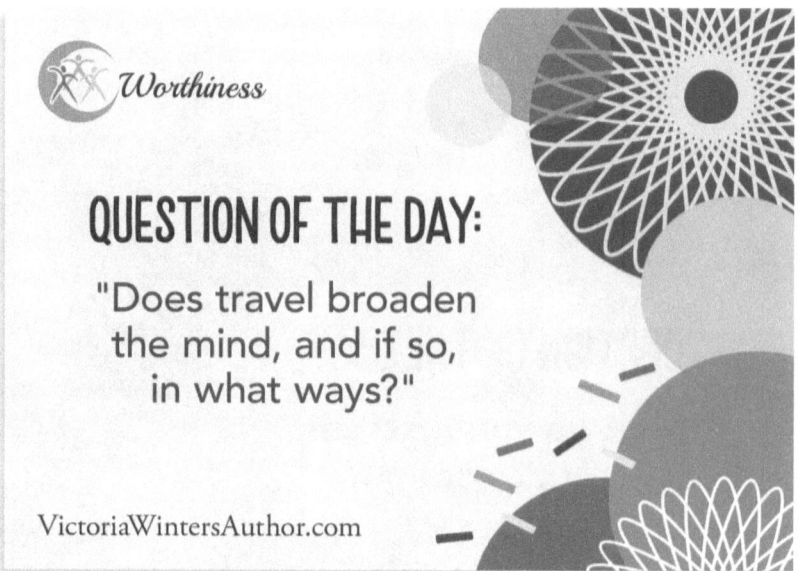

"Common sense is the knack of seeing things as they are, and doing things as they ought to be done."
—HARRIET BEECHER STOWE

Day 3

"If you want to live a long, healthy, and prosperous life, make a commitment to yourself to always be of good cheer. It will affect everything and everyone around you."
—Bill Gove

Day 4

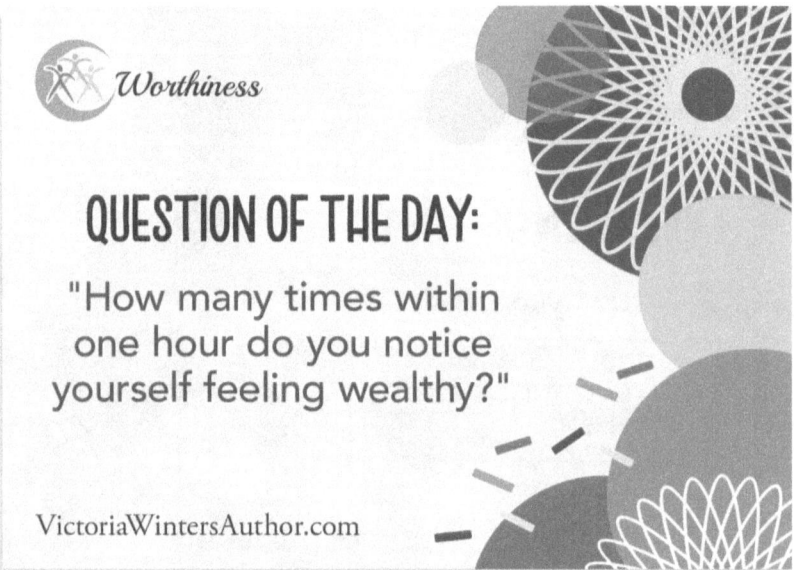

"It is a fundamental fact of life that you can succeed best and quickest by helping others to succeed."
—Napoleon Hill

Day 5

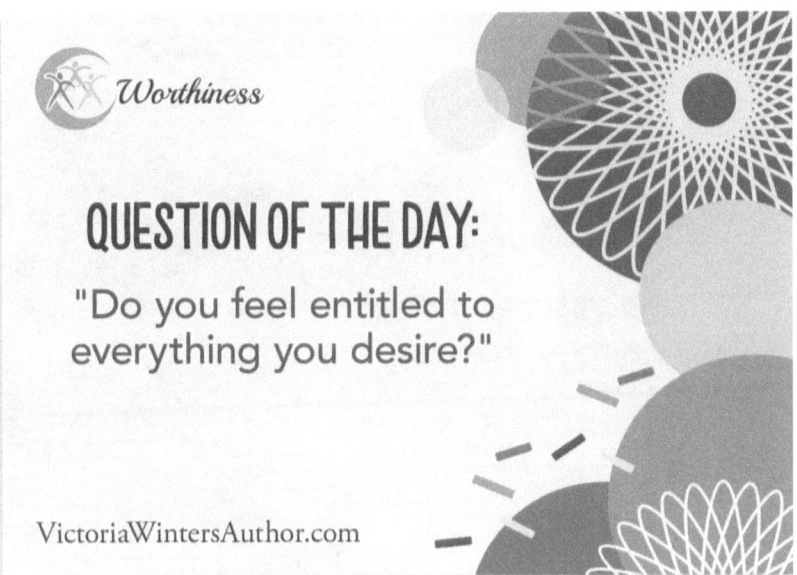

"Desire springs from the awareness of ultimate attainment and that persistence in maintaining the consciousness of the desire already being fulfilled results in its fulfillment."
—NEVILLE

Day 6

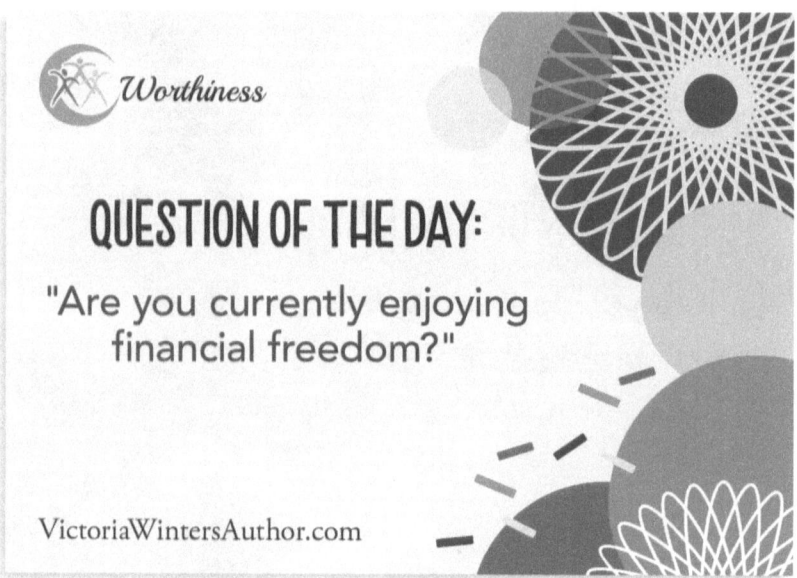

"To live is so startling it leaves little time for anything else."
—Emily Dickinson

Day 7

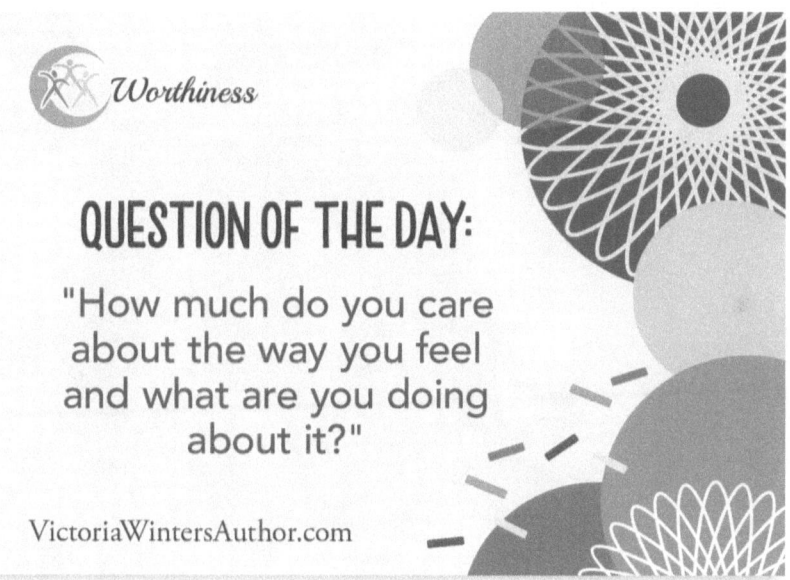

"Everybody is a genius. But, if you judge a fish by its ability to climb a tree, it will live its whole life believing that it is stupid."
—Albert Einstein

Raise your awareness of the good you deserve—ask yourself questions about the beliefs you hold!

chapter three

LOVE AND ORIGINALITY– THE MAGNIFICENT YOU

"Build thee more stately mansions, O my soul,
As the swift seasons roll!
Leave thy low-vaulted past!
Let each new temple, nobler than the last,
Shut thee from heaven with a dome more vast!
Till thou at length art free,
Leaving thine outgrown shell by life's unresting sea!"
—Oliver Wendell Holmes

You can never outdo you! You are capable of infinite growth. This means your power to create your life experiences is unlimited by virtue of your own consciousness. "Build thee more stately mansions," means to imagine more, to think bigger. Your best ideas are for you to enjoy now. Decide to fall in love. Fall in love with your ideas, your plans and above all, love yourself and another person. Love encompasses all and infuses every aspect of life with livingness and purpose.

Life is as beautiful as you imagine it to be. Take yourself to where you plan to be by using your imagination. You must feel the truth of your being and let yourself live fully, freely, peacefully and majestically. "To thine own self be true" are words of pure inspiration. There is no other person exactly like you, but every person is exactly the same in terms of the creative mental tools everyone possesses.

In case you are wondering about the creative mental tools you and every other person is born with, here they are: Imagination, Memory, Reason, Will, Perception and Intuition. In the use of these higher mental faculties, you design and create what you want to experience in your physical reality. The five physical senses, sight, hearing, taste, touch and smell are not inherently creative in nature. You can certainly enjoy what you can see, hear, taste, touch or smell. However, you may find yourself in a weakened position if you allow the outside world to control the inner workings of your phenomenal mind. And, you are more likely to move in the opposite direction of your dream because assigning control of your mindful attention to anything outside of you definitely guarantees you will get a different result than the one you may expect. Seek to express the desires that originate from within.

According to Bob Proctor, the master teacher, speaker and author of *You Were Born Rich*, your greatest work will be in the discovery of numerous ways in which to utilize your gift of co-creative power. Take yourself to the beautiful places you belong. Close the door of your mind while you are inside of your divine imagination. Allow nothing from the outside world to enter or disturb your inner sanctum sanctorum. This is your creative place. It is here your plans can be visualized in full completion, and it is here that you must dwell more often.

Although easier said than done, your real work in life is the pursuit of your own happiness. The most outstanding reason the pursuit of happiness may appear like an ardent chore has a lot to do with the amount of time and energy you spend observing things you do not want. Without a doubt, the real key to enjoying life is to become interested in enjoying your life. What would really knock your socks off?

By paying close attention to the signals of your emotions, you can understand, with absolute precision, everything you have ever lived. And with an ease that you may have never before experienced, you can use this new understanding of your emotions to orchestrate a future experience that will please you in every way.

DISCOVER YOUR OWN MAGNIFICENCE

When you think about "why" you want something, usually your resistance to figuring out how you can get it softens and affords you the comfort of relaxing into blissful thoughts while enjoying your desire. This is one description for the feeling of love. Sensations of light heartedness and effortlessness live on the path of least resistance, which is always open to you. While you enjoy feeling the goodness you rightly deserve, understand that you can capture the essence of a positive feeling. It is a matter of practice.

The only thing that ever causes anyone to feel negative emotion is losing the connection to who they really are. You are magnificent in your uniqueness to fully express your unity with the livingness of life from your point of view. In your thoughts, do you find yourself believing that many good things you want require a lot of work for you to acquire? Do you think that you must fight for what you want because this is the only way? Do you believe that some things are completely out of your reach by virtue of some pre-existing condition?

Here is good news. Love is unconditional unless you choose to place a condition upon it. Being in love is one of the easiest things you can do because love encompasses all and is therefore present everywhere all the time. Conditional love is unnecessary. Apart from the fact that it does not serve you or the person who places a condition upon giving love, you always have a choice to comply or not. A condition for love resembles words like this: *If you would just be compliant and follow this condition, then we are able to love you. If you do this, exactly according to what we say, then we will love you. Otherwise there is no love that we can bestow upon you. In other words, you are toast.*

Freedom is a feeling connected with the activity of choosing what you want to do and experience. If you choose to live your life as an abundant and powerful creator, by all means, practice being the person you imagine yourself to be. You are the only one inhabiting your body and therefore you are in full control of your imagination and other mental faculties. To think a lovely thought is an activity that only you can choose to do for yourself. No matter what you may currently observe or believe, nothing outside of you has the power to think for you. No one can live your wonderful life for you.

There are two parts to everything, the essential and the incidental. These two parts make the difference in every outcome. At one time in my life I worked for a company as a sales representative. This particular position required me to meet hefty quarterly sales objectives. Beside simply asking my clients for orders, I possessed the option to soften my approach by entertaining them. Sometimes the most important thing in a whole day is the rest we take between two deep breaths. Perks and incentives often make the sales process more enjoyable, and I think it is fun to come up with new ways to show people how much you care about them as people, friends and colleagues.

Beyond lunches and the occasional dinner, I could also organize trips and group events for a client and their employees to enjoy. A round of golf ranked high on the list, especially if it meant going to an exclusive and expensive course. The marketing department in my company regularly organized golf tournaments and the sales personnel could choose to invite their clients to attend. Normally I would ask someone from marketing to attend golf tournaments in my place and opt for different events to attend with some of my clients. The marketing team always enjoyed attending their own events if for no other reason than to get out of the office and enjoy the perks of their own design.

For one upcoming golf tournament I could not find anyone available to attend in my place. I went to my boss and asked him to take my place; however, he was otherwise engaged. He asked me why I could not attend with my client. I told him; "I do not play golf. Therefore, I usually assign someone else to go to the golf tournaments in my place." He looked directly into my eyes and said, "That sounds like a personal problem to me. Plan to take your client to the tournament because there in no one else available." Stunned and feeling a bit caught off guard, I assured him that I would take care of my problem, attend the event and quickly left his presence.

"In all our affairs there are two factors, ourselves and the matter to be dealt with; and since for us the nature of anything is always determined by our thought of it, it is entirely a question of our belief which of these two factors shall be the essential and which the accessory. Whichever we regard as the essential, the other at once becomes the incidental."
—THOMAS TROWARD

Knowing that I had to come up with a solution to my personal problem, I decided to begin by thinking about things that I like about golf. To walk through a lovely garden and occasionally hit a little white ball felt like something I was capable of doing. Although I realize that golf is a lot more intricate than a stroll through a park, it felt good to reduce my problem to something simple. Also, knowing there is nothing I would gain by dwelling on something that feels bad other than the acquisition of more bad feelings, I decided a problem is best solved by readily enjoying the solution.

While thinking about a beautiful golf course, my mind drifted toward different, equally delightful thoughts. I like golf attire because it is tasteful and colorful, and it appeals to my sense of understated elegance. I decided to find the best golf outfit for the occasion. Besides, I believed a little retail therapy could do wonders for my mood. From my viewpoint, I knew that if I looked the part, surely, I could play the part.

With a little more than a month to prepare for the tournament, it did not take long for me to find several outfits that I absolutely loved. It also felt exciting to see myself dressed as a golfer. Although, up to this point I had never actually visited a golf course, it dawned on me that I could easily go to one and check it out. Envisioning that it would be a good idea to go to a course that is on par with the one I invited my clients to attend, I selected one to visit in an exclusive area that overlooks the Pacific Ocean. This golf course is best described as a delux oceanfront golf resort with Italian-inspired bungalows and villas, plus dining and a day spa.

While driving through the magnificent entrance of the golf resort, I quietly muttered to myself; "This will do nicely for my introduction to the world of golf." I pulled into an open area where a valet cheerfully waved me toward his podium. Offering a smile as the valet opened my car door, I stepped out feeling completely comfortable within the impressive grounds. I am now often amused that valet parking no longer bothers me ever since I graduated to owning a car worthy of me.

Upon entering the pro shop, I marveled at the luxurious golf attire and accessories. A discrete sign hanging above the check-out counter advertised registration for tee times. Hmm ... What did that mean? Before I allowed myself to listen to unpleasant thoughts reflecting lack of knowledge, I headed straight to the counter to inquire about golf lessons. I told the man behind the counter that I wanted to quickly learn how to play golf. Before I could change my mind, I had a private golf instructor and a month-long schedule for daily lessons. I would begin the next day.

Understanding the difference between *essential* versus *incidental* will help you avoid giving attention to things that you do not want. To give your energy to something you do not want is subtle and deeply ingrained within nearly every person simply because it is practiced daily. You can never escape from having to select your essential and your incidental factors. It is the essential factor, thought, that your attention flows to, as an energizing force that causes the attraction of incidental things, effects, to come to you. Clearly it is within your power to think about what you want and to give energy to it. And by paying attention to the way you feel, you will always know where you stand in relation to the object of your desire.

My first golf lesson surprised me because it began on the driving range. My instructor guided me through an explanation about each golf club, and I practiced hitting the ball. I learned straight away that it is possible to miss striking a stationary object. Humbling and fun, golf lessons reminded me about the importance of focus, by keeping my eye on the ball, and patience. Taking your time to make smooth continuous movements works a lot better than force and over exertion. I diligently practiced and thoroughly enjoyed every lesson.

The golf instructor told me that our last session would take place on the golf course and he would even be my caddie. Definitely, this would be the most exciting of all the lessons and probably the defining factor in my choice to continue to practice and improve. It is often said that golf is addictive and I'm inclined to agree. Golf is primarily a mind game you play on a course with other people in a peaceful and beautiful setting. You can even play a single game by yourself.

The object of the game is to finish with the lowest score below par for the course. Each of the eighteen holes has an assigned number of strokes you can take to sink the ball in the cup on each green. If you take more strokes than the assigned par number, your score increases. As you proceed around the course, you will find opportunities and obstacles that are both interesting and challenging. For example, on a par 5 hole, if it takes you 7 strokes to sink the ball, you have increased your score by 2. However, as you proceed, you can lower your score by sinking your ball in under the par number for a particular hole. The other players present, as fellow companions, also play the course with the similar objective of lowering their score. Every player has fun sharing in the comradery and entertainment each person offers along the way. The best part about golf is that the ultimate prize is what you decide it shall be for yourself.

The day arrived for the tournament. Sporting one of my best outfits, I walked up to the awaiting party of men with a bright smile and the outward appearance of a confident pro. One of the men complimented me and said, "Nice outfit, you look like a pro!" Then he asked me how long I had been playing golf? In that instant I melted inside my head in search of an interesting response, but I immediately remembered that the truth will set me free. Laughing a little, I told him I had just completed one month of golf instruction and this is my first, official round of golf. I also mentioned that I would do my best to keep up with his experienced pace.

Of course, I was terrified to tee off and doubly so as the ladies' tee is positioned forward of the men's tee. This means that I get to watch the men execute their respective shots before moving on to the ladies' tee off position. All three of the men hit their golf balls expertly. As each man made his respective shot, we shouted and cheered as if to help the flying ball soar further and land in a perfect location closer to the green. The time arrived to move ahead to the forward tee for my turn. Standing before three men eagerly waiting to watch me hit my first shot, the little voice inside of me started to scream: "It's your turn, so what are you going to do with three pairs of eyes staring you down?"

Author Thomas Troward eloquently describes the importance of understanding the true position (order) our thoughts must follow to produce the outcome you truly desire. *"For any sort of action to take place there must be some conditions under which the activity passes out into visible results; but the same sort of activity may occur under a variety of different conditions and may thus produce very different visible results. So, in every matter we shall always find an essential or energizing factor and an incidental factor which derives its quality from the nature of the energy."* In other words, it is vitally important to consider the result you want, and give your energy and attention to that result as opposed to giving in to the distracting thoughts that will surely take you in the opposite direction and render an unexpected outcome.

In a moment of absolute clarity, I stepped up, addressed the ball, visualized it making contact with the club and imagined it soaring straight down the fairway. I began by moving my feet from side to side to cause the cleats on the bottom of my shoes to steady my stance. Recalling the words of my instructor, I fixed my eyes on one dimple on the ball's surface, inhaled a refreshing breath of air, relaxed and executed my swing. I could literally feel a warm surge of energy flowing from me and streaming down through the club as it made contact with the tiny object directly on the sweet spot of my attention. For a few heart beats I had completely forgotten about the three pairs of eyes gazing in my direction until I heard the men's voices cheering after I completed my shot. I looked up to watch the ball flying straight down the fairway and make landfall in the middle of the green grassy lane.

Exhaling the super charged emotions built up during the swing of the golf club, I quietly realized I had let go of the anxiety I held about three men watching me make my first drive. As quickly as it began, I freed myself from allowing an imagined obstacle to get in my way. Gosh it feels fantastic to understand that you really can get out of your own way by merely focusing on something you want. Needless to say, my subsequent shots during the eighteen holes on the course landed in various positions that necessitated far more attempts above par to reach the hole, but that is beginner's golf. I intended to have a good time, participate with my clients and end the outing with a feeling of good will and a job well done. Also, it certainly felt marvelous to know that my sales quota was in the bag.

"Excellence may be difficult to define, but we all know it when we see it. It's the sure touch of pride and craftmanship; the unique stamp of personal artistry; the stubborn search for world-class quality, service, teamwork and value." —UNKNOWN

WILL YOU COMMIT TO CELEBRATE EVERY ASPECT OF THE MAGNIFICENT PERSON INSIDE OF YOU?

There is no such thing as partial wholeness. What you really are, in essence, is a concentration of the one universal life spirit expressed into conscious individuality. If you live from the recognition of this truth as your starting point, it makes you free.

One of the mental tools human beings can use to express and experience life on their terms is to use will power effectively. You choose the combinations of thoughts to express and experience in a variety of situations, circumstances and physical things in your own life. And you exercise will power in order to hold thoughts about things you want in your conscious awareness. You are completely free to do whatever your chosen thought combinations move you to do. Better stated, the power you possess to choose something you really want is entirely up to you. Either hold on to those thoughts or dismiss them from your mind.

Napoleon Hill, author of *Think and Grow Rich,* wrote extensively about the power of thought. *"Remember, no more effort is required to aim high in life, to demand abundance and prosperity, than is required to accept misery and poverty."* Bluntly stated, it's exclusively your choice to think about what you want and to go for it, or to focus on things you do not want and suffer the consequences.

Very few things in life improve by themselves. People never improve unless they look to some standard or example higher or better than themselves. Of all human resources, the most precious is the desire to improve if for no other reason than it feels good. By the same token, it is important to understand and believe that no person is better than another. We all simply do things differently because we want to experience different results.

An often misunderstood quality of freedom resides in the action of letting go. To give way to another person, even if you believe them to be incorrect, will set you free to move out of your own way. The emotion of love emphasizes and develops the artistic nature of human beings. Within your quest for increased prosperity, it is easier to tread lightly in the presence of another person by offering them an opportunity to enter into the spirit of a mutually beneficial action or conversation. Give to every person you encounter a subliminal message that embodies the golden rule: "Do unto others as you would have them do unto you."

All living creatures are subject to the law of growth. This means expanding and advancing and becoming something more, bigger and better. An impression of increase in the livingness of life that you feel inside your dreams for an improved or better lifestyle can be projected upon others as an earnest gift you willingly give for their mutual advancement. Walk proudly and delight in the understanding that you are advancing and floating effortlessly in a constant stream of abundant prosperity. *"Whatever you are, be a good one."*—ABRAHAM LINCOLN. Your overflow will shower everyone in your outreach and contribute to their advancing prosperity. Generosity of love and kindness tends to attract the same to the initial giver.

We all desire more fulness of life, a greater and brighter vitality in ourselves and less restriction in our surroundings. Try to learn this lesson: Pay close attention to the things you observe outside of your imagination and notice how you feel. You can cause anything you want to become your experience or possession if you are willing to control your thoughts. It is therefore completely unnecessary that you should seek to rule or control another individual. You waste your efforts and literally create a resistant force that will lead you astray. No matter your profession, religion or position in society, if you give increase to others and make them sensible of the fact, they will be attracted to you and you will prosper beyond your wildest dreams.

"To succeed, try to see how much you can give for a dollar, instead of how little you can give for a dollar."—HENRY FORD.

The things you see outside of your own imagination are manifestations of thoughts and ideas originated by other people and yourself. If this comes as a surprise to you, look around. Are the objects present because you brought them into the space? Or, have you taken yourself to this particular location because you love the idea of occupying a portion of the space? Find something that makes you smile and congratulate yourself. You can always give yourself and others the best experience if you practice guarding your thoughts, words and actions by checking in with yourself for a harmonious and peaceful connection within your marvelous mind. Adopt an attitude of willingness to do things that guarantee your connection with the good you deserve and keep the connection strong.

BELIEVE—while others doubt,
PLAN—while others play,
STUDY—while others delay,
PREPARE—while others day dream,
BEGIN—while others procrastinate,
WORK—while others wish,
INVEST, while others waste,
LISTEN—while others talk,
SMILE—while others frown,
COMMEND—while others criticize,
PERSIST—while others quit.

WHAT DOES LOVE HAVE TO DO WITH LIFE?

Great love surrounds you, and you can tune into it at any time. What life means to you is determined, not so much by what life brings to you, but rather your reaction to what happens. Self-control is an attitude of confidence in your ability to direct your thoughts toward things you want to achieve and experience in your own slice of physical reality. *"Most people never run far enough on their first wind to find out they've got a second. Give your dreams all you've got and you'll be amazed at the energy that comes out of you."*—WILLIAM JAMES

First and foremost, you must love *you*. It is not possible to feel good if you do not love yourself and that includes every aspect of your life. When you have joyful thoughts, amazing wellness, and feel unlimited energy surging to and through you, you are on the frequency of absolute love. This frequency is directly in tune with all the love available to you because you are a magnificent human being created in the image of goodness. To solve any problem you think you have, look directly at the good things you can see within the solution. Seek and ye shall find!

EXERCISE:

1. Write yourself a love letter. You deserve to hear what you think about you from the third person voice. Write an unabashedly passionate letter dripping with the gushiness of romantic love.
2. Describe what you love about the person you are becoming and the way you contribute to living life to the fullest.
3. Tell a boastful story about an accomplishment you achieved that boldly speaks about the greatness you continuously bring to the world.
4. Step into the essence of who you are and pour your heart out about the power you brandish in shaping life according to your own ideas.
5. Surprise yourself as you describe the way you would be introduced to anyone that you admire or imagine to be great. If done correctly, you will enter into the spirit of your own life and realize that everything you write is an existing truth within you.

6. Be magnificent, have a really good time and then read it aloud. Let your last sentence state: "I am magnificent and I expect to be with *you* throughout my life."

Love is often measured by the intensity of a feeling and apportioned into categories. You may have heard phrases like, "I love him like a brother," or "I really like her a lot", or "That is something I would love to acquire." News flash: There is only love. The intensity of your feelings, if carefully observed, will guide you toward thinking about things you want more often. Is there any reason you would give the time of day to think about something that is not lovely while you are feeling really good? And if so, how would that serve you in the best way?

You release energy and love in much the same way that you receive it. This is an effortless process unless you believe you must do something strenuous to acquire either one. If you could acquire more energy and love in a way that feels effortless, would you seek to find the method to employ? Of all the choices you can make, choose to understand that there are no limits to energy and love. As a super human being, you simply cannot run out of energy any more than you can avoid the experience of love manifesting throughout your miraculous life.

"The essence of life is movement of beautiful energy encapsulated in an atom of pure love ever ready for expansion into your personal reality."
—Victoria Winters

LIVE AS IF YOU ARE THE PERSON YOU WOULD LOVE TO MEET.

Open your heart and believe that you get better all the time. True happiness and being in love with your life will sustain you throughout your days. To have fun and savor happiness are close but not exactly the same. True happiness is something that functions deep within your being and it is long-lasting. Fun, a lot of the time can feel shallow and may evaporate before it has time to circle around and compel you to do it again. Having fun is a decision you can make and compel it to move with you from task to task. Deciding to enjoy everything you do will open your mind and allow more ideas to flow to you that you can act upon. Essentially, this makes life more enjoyable because you are in control.

For the most part, people become products of their past thinking. Many of the beliefs held in the mind are absurd. The power of suggestion is a mighty force and often triggers an action to stop yourself before you begin. You know how it goes … "what would people think if I did that?"

Your memory is perfect as evidenced by your ability to instantly flash a deeply held belief to your present consciousness that will cause you to feel a certain way. What you say about yourself is music to your ears, unless you are off key. Being off key is much like doing something you really do not want to do, but you do it anyway because it is familiar. This doesn't sound or feel good and neither does listening to a trio of singers when one member is out of tune.

Moving to a new city can be thrilling, especially when you do not know many people who live in the area. On one such occasion I found myself accepting an opportunity to move abroad for a period of time. As an avid reader and writer, it is particularly easy for me to imagine scenes and different scenarios in which to place myself. Having travelled vicariously as a fictionalized character in many a novel, it became time for me to actually become the person I would like to meet.

My nameless heroes are people who travel and move around the world exploring life with the expectation of enjoying luxuriously comfortable surroundings, meeting new friends, lending a hand and spreading joy while having the time of their lives. A charmed life comes to mind as the perfect description for what I am certain you would love to experience in your world.

During my days in high school, an English teacher introduced our class to the idea of corresponding with fellow students who resided in different countries around the world. Learning to describe my student life and activities of personal interest to another person by writing to them helped tremendously to improve my attention to otherwise boring lessons in grammar. Somewhere along the way I found myself keenly interested in language structure and also in learning multiple languages. I became fascinated with reading the points of view about life from the perspective of people who live in different areas of the world. In principle, I really love to look at happenings in life and to see things I would like to experience in my own world. What about you? Do you dream vividly and see yourself doing something different?

Well, beyond my high school days and into college I continued to correspond with my distant friends. Writing letters and, better yet, receiving hand-written letters continued to hold my fascination and desire for new travel adventures. I wanted to see the world and to meet some of the people I had been writing to over the years. As a college student it had not occurred to me that I could simply take off on a jet plane and visit any place I desired because I had no idea how I could pull that off. However, undeterred, I held on to the intention to take those trips while I continued to correspond.

Often, I would feel as if I were a stranger among my own circle of friends. In other words, I felt unwilling to participate in some of the conversations that did not feel good to me. Nor did I believe many concepts spoken about to actually be true. Moreover, I simply could not understand many invisible fears people would speak about that stopped them from even imagining something more wonderful for themselves. As far as I knew, the things I would think about felt so good that I became drawn to exploring new opportunities. After all, it cost next to nothing to read brochures and plan trips. And it was certainly easy enough to explore new places of interest even though the images were only photographs in a travel brochure.

People are everywhere and it is easy to speak to any person if you are willing to smile and utter a greeting. Chances are a smile and a compliment are just the things that will open a new door for you. In many instances, a thought about the lack of money is the only thing that stops a person from taking action. You do not need money to imagine. You do not need money to explore a new idea unless and until you are ready to purchase something. You become ready to take action by thinking about what you really want, making plans and working your plan.

Facts are only accepted fiction. You are taught to believe certain ideas are hard facts and the large mass of individuals in any given area readily accept certain ideas from others as indisputable gospel. You can believe or change your beliefs at any moment. You are not at the mercy of anyone's ideas unless you believe you are. You can change any belief and free yourself from limitation within the frame work of your own dreams. What do you want that you believe you cannot have? It is your *belief* about not having what you want that manifests lack in your physical reality.

Many people tend to focus too much on being tough and tolerating pain, discomfort and discontent. We lose touch with the fact that our discontent actually points to something we need to change in our lives. "No pain, no gain" can be viewed as an opportunity to look for something that feels better while in the midst of experiencing something to the contrary. As you move through and away from where you have just been, notice the fork in the road at your disposal.

The pursuit of happiness is a call from a voice inside of you that urges you to expand your own greatness by doing things you love. *"If a person advances confidently in the direction of their dream and endeavors to live the life they have imagined, they will meet with success unexpected in common hours."*—HENRY DAVID THOREAU

There is something so very special about you. You can only expand whatever you give attention to because energy is a life-giving force you direct in every moment. This life-giving force is always with you, so direct it well. Understand, while streaming your attention to the good you desire, you will attract everything you require to help you reach your goal effortlessly. Feel good. You'll be so glad you did!

"Where there is sterling faith and uncompromising purity there is health, there is success, there is power. In such a one, disease, failure and disaster can find no lodgment, for there is nothing on which they can feed."
—JAMES ALLEN

part two
CLARITY

chapter four

TO BE—FREEDOM AND OTHER MIRACULOUS IDEAS

*"The difference between fiction and reality?
Fiction has to make sense."*
—Tom Clancy

OF ALL THE noteworthy ideas on earth, freedom must rank at the top of the list as the most sought out concept by people around the globe. What exactly is freedom? A dictionary definition will offer various explanations based on usage in language and sentence structure. It may even attempt to assist a reader's understanding by presenting contextual scenarios that describe the absence of freedom.

Countries, governments, communities and other groups announce their personal and collective definitions of freedom along with a strong emphasis about how your personal liberty will become compromised. People in many countries have specific definitions and rules about religious and political rights as prescribed by authoritarian leaders. These leaders are often the source of curtailed freedom. It is also common to find "unwritten social rules" that dictate an absolute compliance for members of a particular social group as established by members of a community. Many of these obvious restrictions to personal freedom of expression or participation in common activities are based on restrictive criteria.

Whatever your definition of freedom, know that your freedom to think your own thoughts is guaranteed simply because you are alive. All living human beings naturally possess absolute freedom of thought. As quiet as it is kept, you are the only person who can limit the amount of freedom you are able to enjoy by the thoughts you entertain.

You are free to choose whatever you want to think about at any moment. You are free to do whatever you want to do based on your beliefs about doing certain things. Above all, you are free to change your mind. And even if you possess beliefs held for decades or minutes, you are the only person who changes your own mind.

Theoretically you are the center of your own world. Even during times when you allow images of other people, circumstances, situations or any memory of a past event to temporarily intrude upon your personal space, you remain free and in charge of your life. You can introduce a new thought to a past event and completely change the outcome of any story. It matters not that an event you rearrange only happened mentally because this is an activity inside your mind that you can develop and experience as a new future event if you so desire. Subsequently, this begs the question: How real is reality?

EXERCISE:

1. Given the above question to be an interesting one to ask yourself, take a moment to describe the realness of your current reality. Include in your description exactly what makes any particular reality real for you.
2. As you think about your answer, pay close attention to the way you feel. If you are willing to visualize yourself as the "Star" in a feature film, write about what the "Star" is doing to entertain the viewers in present tense.

Life under your control feels good. To clearly see what you want to see and to move toward it confidently with a full expectation of receiving it will liberate and renew your thriving inner spirit. You should aim to always be on your own side and in harmony with whatever you desire. When you fight with yourself about anything you want, who wins? For that matter, who loses?

Many times I have started a fight with myself not understanding that I actively chose to engage in conflicts with myself. However, to realize every person often makes this type of choice multiple times during a day and throughout many years proves to be an eye-opener and quite an amusing revelation. On one such occasion I happened to be sitting in my car in front of my place of employment. As a matter of routine, I would arrive early enough to finish drinking a cup of coffee and compose my thoughts before entering the work place. Perplexingly, the majority of my thinking had nothing to do with the pending work agenda awaiting my attention.

With warm coffee surging through my system, it surprised me to feel only marginally prepared to step out and participate in the office environment. I mused: "I am here now and it is best to just get in there and get the job over with as soon as possible." However, in a moment of hesitation I noticed that I could not open the car door. Nothing physically blocked my hand except a tiny voice that whispered; "Hold on for a minute." Indulging myself, I relaxed, inhaled silently and decided to capitalize on the benefit of listening to the inner conversation. I became fascinated with exploring the ideas fluttering around inside my head and it behooved me to take my time. After all, to hurry into the office provided me no extra benefit and certainly no extra money, so I extended latitude to this rather bizarre sensation.

Sitting quietly and feeling a bit foolish, once again I lifted my hand to guide it to the door handle and once more it met with resistance. My hand, mysteriously redirected, landed firmly on the steering wheel. For sure I knew something peculiar was going on, and I believed I merely needed to relax and wait for the feeling to pass. Instead of relaxing, an even stronger impulse urged me to start the engine and return home. The longer I sat behind the steering wheel, the more I wanted to escape the parking lot and drive until I felt secure enough to stop and exit my vehicle.

Whether or not anyone could determine that I might be experiencing an anxiety attack or just a moment of temporary insanity remains unknown. With a clear vision of my intentions, I reminded myself that I should pay attention to my feelings and avoid going against the strong urge that compelled me to remain buckled in my seat. I sat perfectly still looking out of the window like a cat observing the world from a perch lodged against a window. My own words further reminded me that I had all the time in the world and I deserved to use a few moments to gather my composure before heading into the office.

During my standstill, pleasant thoughts danced across the screen of my mind. I thought about what I would do if I decided to play hooky from work. Pangs of pleasure hit me like rockets nudging me to step on the accelerator and take off. A full-blown discussion about the pros and cons of taking an unplanned day off whirled around my mind. With no end to my own "What if?" questions, I got paper out and started to write my ideas for and against going into the office. You probably can come up with your own list of pros and cons about taking an unscheduled day off work. This would give you a firsthand account of the ping pong game I played in the car.

Writing a list helped me uncover some unfounded fears that simply made no sense. Nothing would overtly change in my lifestyle by skipping a day of work. I surmised I would still have a roof over my head, plenty to eat, drink and enough money to meet my ongoing obligations. Whether or not the boss would survive a day without my participation did not bother me. Everyone is replaceable and I knew that I would always find work if I wanted to look for a different job.

The evidence of a woman in conflict with herself became apparent to me as I sat alone in my car. No one stood outside my door and neither did anyone call out to me and demand that I go inside the building. I began to understand that I am the only person truly capable of stopping myself and therefore the only one who can jump start myself into action. In a flash, I completely abandoned the idea of entering the building; I started the car and drove home.

Instantly I began to breathe easier and the uncomfortable feelings drifted effortlessly out of my mind. Still thinking about my pros and cons list, I started to pinch off the cons and sent them on their way. I no longer seemed to care about reliving the anxiety that got me moving off my predetermined plan of going to work. All I really wanted at this time was to feel better and that became the object of my attention.

Once at home I rang my mother to seek her advice about how to handle speaking with my boss about my spontaneous day off. Among other things, I did not want to report to the office that I simply did not feel like going to work nor pretend that I suddenly became ill and needed to use a sick day. Something inside of me would perpetually ignite a feeling of awkwardness when faced with a directive to do something that I did not want to do.

For some inexplicable reason, it seemed to me that throughout life people are constantly encouraging others to do things they really do not want to do for the purpose of pleasing someone else. You may be familiar with these commonly held beliefs. *"Pay no attention to how you feel, just follow orders and handle yourself. You wouldn't want people to think of you as rebellious or a trouble maker. If you want to get somewhere in life you have to do things you do not like from time to time. You must follow certain rules. There will always be people in higher places that know what is best for you. Life is just this way and there is nothing you can do about it."*

Words to this effect have never made a lot of sense to me, but on the other hand, I have never spoken to anyone directly about my thoughts on the subject. And this includes allowing myself to contemplate the reason I would allow myself to feel compelled to do something I do not enjoy.

Fortunately, my mother can see the humor in situations that would normally bring out the worst in a person. A positive attitude is essential whenever you find yourself involved with solving a problem that you think is holding you back from doing something you would love. When you give attention and energy to something you do not want, it is like pouring gasoline on a fire. It inflames, gets bigger and eventually consumes everything in the surrounding area. My mother understood immediately that I probably did not like my job and she gently asked me: "What do you really want to do?"

In the midst of searching for a response to her question, many thoughts entered my mind and for the most part it would have been impolite to share some of my thoughts about how I really felt about my job. With the presence of mind to accurately answer her question, I told her I did not know exactly, but I would like to take a break, relax and go on an excursion.

Instinctively, we both knew my days were numbered for continuing with the current employer, but meanwhile, I needed to make some decisions. To this day I remain grateful for our conversation, her kind words and the laughter we shared about the drama I concocted just to get myself moving in a different direction. And it is also nice to learn that parents eventually do become friends and confidants.

I spent several hours planning a trip to San Francisco while dreaming about the experience I really wanted to enjoy. I never got around to calling the office to let the boss know I would not be coming in to work. I promised myself that for this one day I would only pay attention to feeling good and think about things that I really wanted to do. I made it my mission to place myself in an ideal situation and experience every detail in the present moment. Literally, I commanded myself to defy present circumstances and to see only what I wanted to see. I allowed nothing to thwart my pleasure and to my surprise I knew with absolute certainty that I would re-experience my daydream in physical reality.

With regard to treating people the way you would have them treat you, I knew any explanation I could offer for not going to work would be better left unsaid. There is another golden rule I decided to use on this particular day; "If you have nothing good to say, keep quiet."

The three days I spent at the Mark Hopkins hotel in San Francisco opened my mind to the idea that I could do anything I wanted to do. I learned that looking at a current situation or circumstance for longer than the present moment is unnecessary because those thoughts will lead you in a circle. Living a joyful life in a constantly moving and evolving world must have something to do with where you choose to place your attention. Concentrating on your desires versus contemplating others' ideas is a profound conclusion. What value is gleaned from dwelling on current evidence contrary to your imagined desire?

It is not the easiest exercise to visualize a perfect scenario without allowing some negative beliefs to slither into the scene. To the exclusion of thoughts that lived on the "pros and cons list," I decided to close the door to those dream killers and stand guard over my true interests. After numerous encounters and sometimes blatant assaults to override my decision hurled at me from my own beliefs, I got better at showing those negative thoughts the backside of the door.

In many respects, you probably have similar stories you can tell about things you accomplished that once felt impossible from where you stood. It is only in looking back that you can account for the steps you took to reach where you stand today.

"Guilt puts you on a treadmill; you're constantly working and struggling and sweating, but you don't move forward."—JOEL OLSTEEN

THE FREEDOM TO MIND YOUR OWN BUSINESS

As an expression, "mind your own business," can be perceived as good advice or an impolite statement if spoken aloud to another person in a raised tone of voice. You always have a choice to examine beforehand the words you intend to use. Whether speaking to yourself or another person, kindness, generosity and gratitude should precede every expression. This may be enhanced by the practice of attending to the business of your own life.

If you have not considered your life as a business you are in charge of operating, you may miss subtle nuances in daily activities that could be used to greater advantage. You will never fail if you never give up. Preoccupation with seeking others' approval coupled with reliving the past will impede your progress toward achieving your desired goal.

Giving yourself a command and following it is a practice you can choose to develop. Would you prefer that another person command you to do something whether you like it or not? And then you spend precious time working to align with something you ultimately do not even want? Being involved with the ideas of others may retard your progress toward achieving your own design. Essentially, you have deviated from going where you want to go, and you will ultimately spend more time aligning with your own idea.

You are an independent individual living in your own body that you have complete dominion over. Another person cannot take control of your body unless you allow it. It is important to understand this simple concept. Even a baby independently operates within its own skin, but needs external help for a period of time to learn its physical capabilities and mental gifts. Once a person reaches the level of maturity and independence, intervention diminishes steadily in the mind of the other person. Even though a child may need further guidance, you have no power to control their thoughts. For the sake of this conversation, parental guidance is excluded from the discussion of minding your own business.

The feeling of having what you desire now is the inner knowing that your desires manifest perfectly in your own physical reality. It is my belief that The Law of Vibration works in conjunction with your thoughts and other universal laws to guarantee manifestation of all things in conscious alignment with the thinker. Upon careful examination of events in your life, understand they are perfect manifestations of the thought mix you provide energy to. Your attention fuels thought movement into your present reality. What could possibly be imperfect about what happens in any given moment?

Perfecting your own living experience has everything to do with managing your thoughts. You are powerless to manage the thoughts of another. You simply have no control over what another person thinks or does. You do not live inside of another person and therefore cannot manage the business of living their life according to the thoughts you may want for them to accept and think about. Quite simply, that is beyond your control. Be free. Let yourself and other people off the hook. Pay attention exclusively to the management of your own life and prosper in the business you choose to create for yourself. If done correctly, you will naturally begin to increase your attention to thoughts in harmony with your ideas and you will also notice the waning enticement of outside distractions. Your life will change before your eyes as you move under the direction of your control.

A person driven by emotional motivators—their dreams, desires and passions—will eventually ask the question: "Why must I suffer?" Developing and clarifying your vision and desires will fill your imagination and deliver new ideas to you like plates passing before you on a conveyor belt. These ideas will be of such a nature that you can easily execute them immediately. And as good as this feels, your outward projection of the person you become will shine brightly for other people to see. Like-minded individuals will enter your sphere of influence because they will naturally gravitate to you. If you need help, you will attract what you require along the way by virtue of the magnetic force pulling from within your creative mind that is focused exclusively upon your dreams.

"Nothing can add more power to your life than concentrating all of your energies on a limited set of targets."—NIDO QUBEIN

The possibilities for enjoying your life are unlimited. You set limitations for yourself by paying attention to beliefs that are in opposition to your desire. The power you possess to live life on your terms is a simple concept. Whether a belief you hold originated from another person's idea or your own makes zero difference in your decision to think about things that please you. You can always change your mind, and there is no one in the world whom you must ask for permission.

> *Mind is the Master power that moulds and makes,*
> *And Man is Mind, and evermore he takes*
> *The tool of Thought, and, shaping what he wills,*
> *Brings forth a thousand joys, a thousand ills;—*
> *He thinks in secret and it comes to pass:*
> *Environment is but his looking-glass.*
> "AS A MAN THINKETH" BY JAMES ALLEN

FREEDOM OF CHOICE—MAKE A DECISION

Among miraculous ideas available to you is your power to choose whatever you want. First, you must decide what you want and immediately claim it as yours. Esther Hicks is the voice for the teachings of a collective entity called Abraham, and she instructs that in the moment you ask, your desire is given. This is especially good news if you choose to believe in the truth of her statement. Ask yourself important questions. "How committed are you to achieving your vision? Are you willing to do what it takes?

For many years I have been involved in personal development and have attended numerous seminars, lectures and read a prodigious amount of related literature. In all honesty, the daily study and discipline required to get to know myself better fascinates me and continues to hold my attention.

To surround yourself with like-minded people definitely helps to maintain the daily disciplines required to grow in awareness, but it is not the only way to live an abundant lifestyle. Your life is under your control and it is therefore necessary to maintain control. This is a matter of personal practice and something anyone can do.

It is a good idea to follow industry leaders in any field you find particularly interesting. Whatever you want to learn or improve upon is accomplished easier with expert guidance. One of the keys to understanding your role in life is to know that you are here primarily to help other people. Yes, you have an obligation to yourself to enjoy your life, but to help others along the way is a side benefit that enhances your own well-being.

I had been following Bob Proctor for a number of years and wanted to attend his seminar called, "Paradigm Shift." When I first heard about it, I decided to purchase a ticket and sit in the VIP section. This seminar was to be the first of its kind and the topic immediately drew people to register quickly.

My husband and I were preparing to vacation on Lake Tahoe which was an eight-hour drive. In my attention to the preparations for our trip, I neglected to register immediately and subsequently let a number of days pass before it occurred to me that I had completely forgotten to sign up and pay for the seminar. I called Bob's office and found out the event was sold out. Hearing this news crashed down on me. The result of my procrastination lay at my feet and there was nothing I could do to create more tickets.

There is one thing I have taken to heart and learned through self-development study. Giving exclusive attention to the desired object requires great practice. In order to override procrastination, take action while an idea is fresh on your mind. I decided to ask about a waiting list.

I had my heart set on going to the event, and I felt as if my life depended on it. I had no idea the reason why I felt so strongly about attending this particular seminar. I politely explained my feelings to the woman on the phone, thanked her for adding me to the wait list and immediately experienced a warm wave of gratitude. The happiest feeling washed over me, and I immediately felt a delicious sense of peace.

From the moment I hung up the phone, I began to think about being in the same room with Bob Proctor and listening to his words of wisdom. I sat quietly for a few minutes and visualized receiving the phone call to register. I gave my full attention to a lively scenario playing in my imagination that felt so vividly real that I noticed goose bumps forming on my skin. To be physically in attendance became a burning desire inside of me and I knew the heat from my glowing inner delight must energetically move like electricity speeds to illuminate a room with the flick of a switch.

Lake Tahoe is a large freshwater lake and resort area that borders California and Nevada. This majestic mountain community becomes a haven for boaters, water skiers, sailors and hikers during the summer months and seasonally transforms into a winter wonderland. Known for its beaches and ski resorts, the Incline Village area, situated approximately 6, 350 feet above sea level, is also home to splendid restaurants, shops, hotels and mountain-chalet-style homes.

Naturally beautiful surroundings in nature have a way of putting a person at ease even in the midst of rapid mental activity that often camouflages internal calmness. I received the call to claim my VIP seat during a leisurely afternoon lunch while overlooking Lake Tahoe.

A journey to any destination begins with an idea and a plan. In preparation for spending a long weekend unaccompanied by a familiar acquaintance, it occurred to me that it would be a good idea to set an intention for the desired outcome of attending the seminar. Again, to ask myself a question that triggers ideas—What do I really want?—I began to think about what I would love to experience.

Throughout your lifetime many people will move in and out of your social spheres. The natural process of growth includes the attrition of friends, family and other acquaintances. It is easy to understand that just as easily as you can outgrow clothing or see machinery diminish in usefulness, you will continue to meet different people and acquire a variety of new and different objects. As much as I expected to attend the seminar, I likewise expected to meet a new friend that would fill an open space in my social sphere.

Observing people in action is often fun and entertaining, especially when you are waiting in a line, seated in an airport or moving around a hotel lobby. It is easy to create stories and to imagine what another person may be on their way to do. I enjoy what I call "the fashion parade" whenever I afford myself the pleasure of searching for the most creative outfits on display.

The weekend of the seminar materialized rather quickly, and I arrived at the hotel one day ahead of schedule. It often feels exciting to be in a different location, and I was ready to take full advantage of spending a little time by myself. Shortly after settling into my hotel room, I decided to walk around and explore the common areas. A nicely dressed woman walking through the hotel lobby appeared to be headed in my direction. Because I was in no particular hurry, I took a moment to watch her successfully maneuver around a few people with her suitcase in tow. She looked happy and walked with a subtle air of confidence that brought a smile to my face.

As the woman came closer to my vicinity, I felt an urge to speak to her. I appreciated the way she carried herself and I thought she deserved to know someone noticed the care she had obviously taken to dress for success. Speaker Les Brown once said: *"No one rises to low expectations."*

Paying no attention to the little voice that told me a number of reasons to remain quiet, I smiled and summoned the courage to tell her how very nice she looked. I loved her color choice of cream and the lace and pearls that accentuated her outfit. She returned a smile and said: "You look very nice too. Look at you; we have on similar style outfits." We laughed and continued on our respective ways in opposite directions. I thought to myself that whatever that woman does for a living must be something totally satisfying. It is not often that I encounter a total stranger and wonder what they do. In this instance, I found the similarity in our attire an amazing coincidence. However, I do not believe in coincidence, so I let the happy encounter continue to float around my mind as a sign of more good things to come over the weekend.

No matter what you are planning to do, you have an opportunity to shine through the clothing you select. It is important to remember that your own magnificence and the way you feel about yourself is more obvious to other people than you probably remember to recall. You may find it of enormous value to permit yourself to pay greater attention to the way you feel.

Inside the ballroom for the seminar, the friendly atmosphere doubled the greeting everyone received as they entered the room. I could feel the collective magnitude of happiness reverberating as people met and greeted others. Not knowing anyone here, I had the opportunity to meet new people and generally circulate in a supercharged, positive atmosphere. To my surprise, the woman I previously met in the lobby stood surrounded by a group of people eagerly engaged in conversation. I had imagined her to be on her way to another destination when we spoke in the lobby only because she had been headed in the general direction of the front door.

Our eyes met and she re-introduced herself to me. Her name—Peggy McColl, New York Times Best Selling Author, speaker and teacher. At this time, I learned she would make a presentation to the audience later on in the day. I was happy to see her again and to re-experience the beautiful self-confident wave of energy she streamed my way. In an inspired moment of clarity, I decided that I would love to get to know Peggy better.

"The deepest principle in human nature is the craving to be appreciated."
—WILLIAM JAMES

THE ULTIMATE GOAL OF FREEDOM—TRUST YOURSELF

Dr. Martin Luther King's famous "I Have A Dream" speech includes three words that are the ultimate instruction about how to realize your own liberty—*"Let freedom ring."* Take a moment to speak those words aloud, and listen for the gentleness contained in the advice.

You are truly magnificent and you already possess everything you could possibly need to enjoy the goodness of any reality you decide to manifest for yourself. As a follow-on to the Golden Rule: "Do unto others as you would have them do unto you," implement a few daily practices.

1. Examine your beliefs by asking yourself questions.
2. Be a good listener.
3. Give to everyone a feeling of importance.
4. Cultivate the habit of being grateful for every good thing that comes to you.
5. Let go of the past. Allow and expect the goodness you deserve.

FORGIVE

"That slight misdeed of yesterday,
why should it mar today?
The thing he said, the thing you did,
have long since passed away;
For yesterday was but a trial;
today you will succeed.
And from mistakes of yesterday
will come some noble deed.

Forgive yourself for thoughtlessness,
do not condemn the past;
For it is gone with its mistakes;
Their mem'ry cannot last;
Forget the failures and misdeed,
from such experience rise,
Why should you let your head be bowed?
Lift up your heart and eyes!"—Unknown

"If you are going to achieve excellence in big things, you develop the habit in little matters. Excellence is not an exception; it is a prevailing attitude."—COLIN POWELL

chapter five

CLARIFY YOUR DESIRE—
ASK AND EXPECT AN ANSWER

Day 1

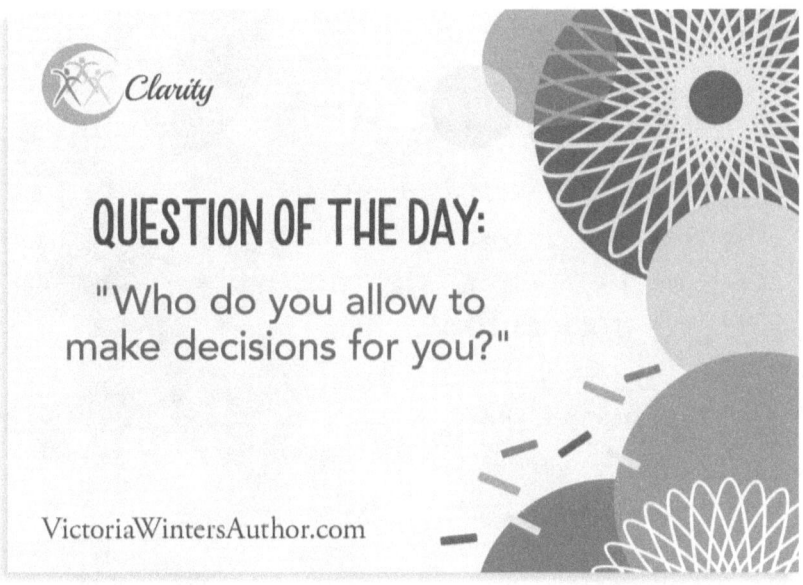

"Perhaps the most valuable result of all education is the ability to make yourself do the thing you have to do, when it ought to be done, whether you like it or not. It is the first lesson that ought to be learned and however early a man's training begins, it is probably the last lesson that he learns thoroughly."
—Thomas Henry Huxley

Day 2

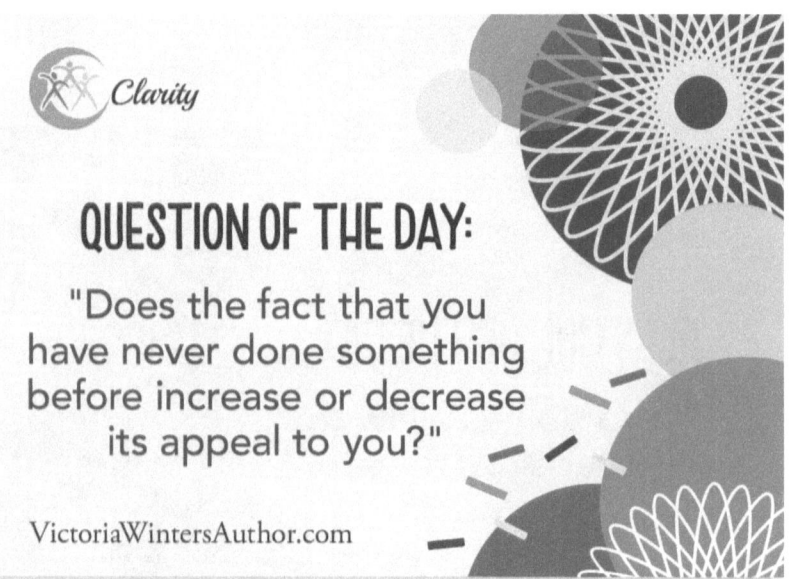

> *"Enlightenment is a state of wholeness, of being "at one" and therefore at peace. At one with life in its manifested aspect, the world, as well as with your deepest self and life unmanifested —at one with Being."*
> —Eckhart Tolle

Day 3

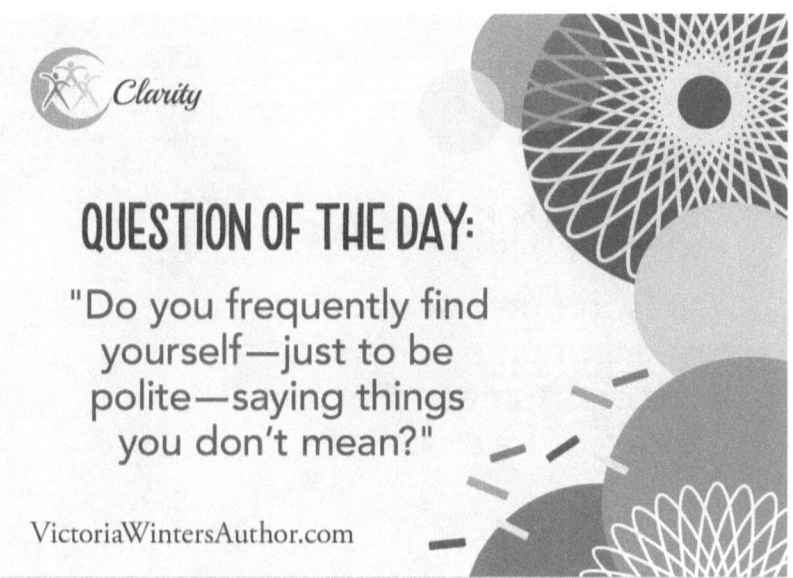

"Living a life that you love and loving the life that you are living is the truest demonstration of abundance."
—LISA NICHOLS

Day 4

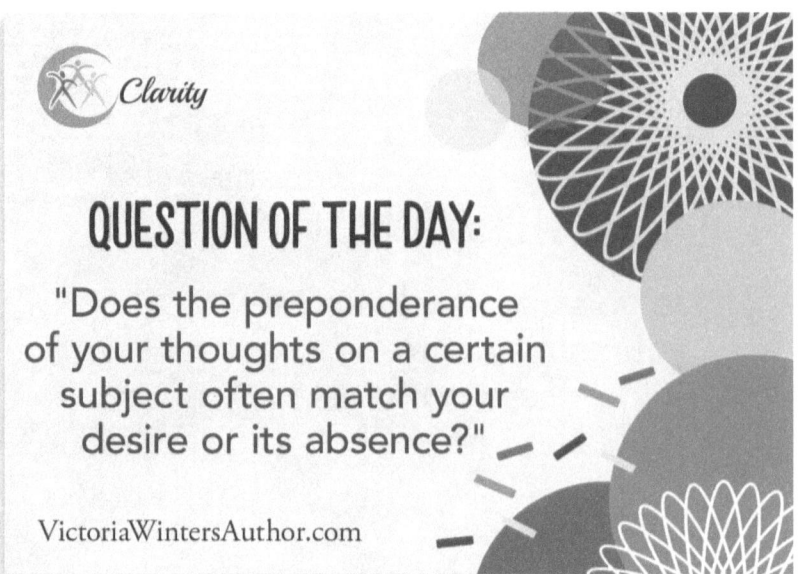

> "Disorder is the ultimate evil. Order is the initial good.
> Only the bored welcome the unexpected. Delight in order.
> Order is the mother of freedom."
> —L. Rust Hills

Day 5

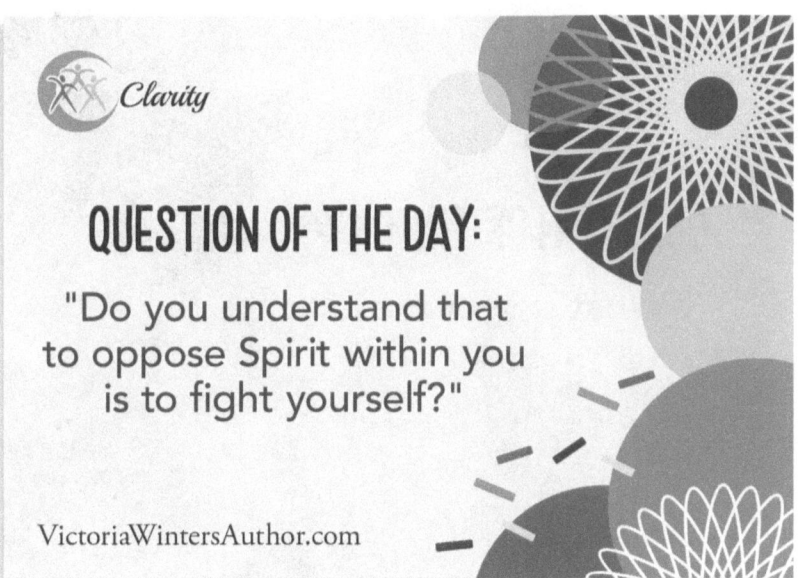

*"How wonderful it is to do your will! For that is freedom.
Unless you do your will you are not free."*
—A Course in Miracles

Day 6

> "Money never made a man happy yet, nor will it.
> There is nothing in its nature to produce happiness."
> —BENJAMIN FRANKLIN

Day 7

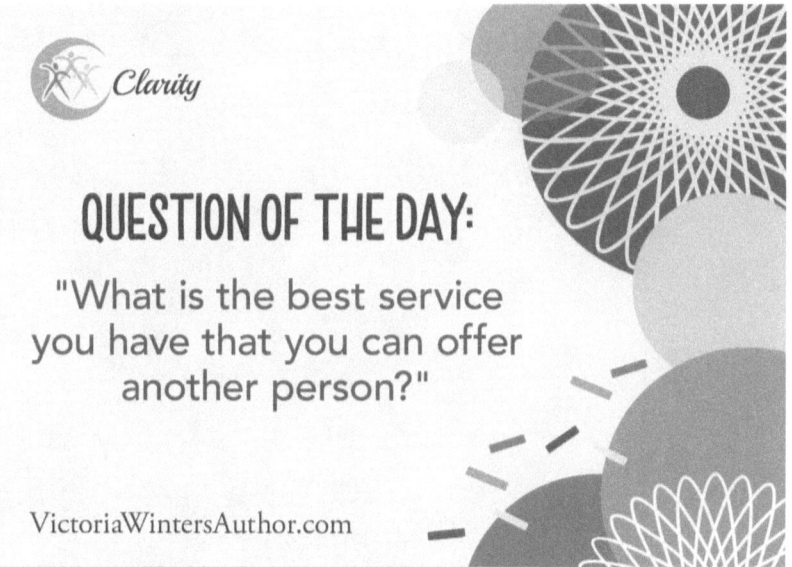

*"Courage is what it takes to stand up and speak;
courage is also what it takes to sit down and listen."*
—Winston S. Churchill

The clearer you see the desire, the closer it is to you!

chapter six

MASTER THE CHOICE TO FEEL GOOD

*"My life is a performance for which I was
never given any chance to rehearse."*
—Ashleigh Brilliant

It is important to realize the wonderful person who populates your body. The very power you seek is in your hands at every moment. You work against yourself whenever you consider things you do *not* want. Giving your attention to anything infuses it with pure, positive energy.

Your results are a natural expansion of whatever receives the energy flow from your attention. And the way you feel is your indicator of the direction in which your energy goes. In essence, you are either creating the exquisite experience of something you adore, or a limited and often vastly different version of your heart's desire. You take yourself forward, toward the thing you want or in a different direction to something you may not recognize or readily expect.

The greater the flow your life-giving energy moves with the intensity of your emotions as you hold focus upon a thought, the larger and stronger it becomes. And by the Law of Attraction, a magnetic force activated by the expansion of a thought, draws 'like kind' thoughts that will be taken up by Spirit to produce the exact circumstances, situations or objects it is called upon to produce in its inherent nature to express itself. Therefore, pay attention to feeling the goodness you desire to expand. —Victoria Winters

The way you feel has everything to do with the physical results you expect to experience. And regardless of whether this sounds like something out of this world, at best, this is a simple explanation of the creative process by which all things become physical manifestations. In the moment the object of your desire becomes clear to you, it is done. At once complete in your mind, the way you feel about your creation is the result you expect and can enjoy immediately.

Initially, your creation is virtually "out of this world" because it first resides in your personal realm of imagination. While basking in the blissful feelings concerning the thing you want, you will naturally move yourself along your path of least resistance as you head toward its physical manifestation. It is much easier to feel good *first* and to allow the conditions, situations and circumstances to present themselves to you rather than to think about how to obtain something you think you do not possess.

Instant physical manifestation eludes everyone. How empowering it is to know that you can change your mind before something automatically appears before your eyes. Because of your ability to choose from an inexhaustible array of thoughts available to you in any given moment, it is possible to speed up manifestations by paying greater attention to the way you feel. The present moment is your time to prepare and to think about getting ready for whatever you want while you ride the emotional wave of bliss and enjoy the sensation of having it now.

Order is the first law of the universe. To illustrate the order of the way thought and feeling work for you before taking action, consider the following premise. If you need a change in condition to feel good, then the condition will be slow in coming, if ever. If you can feel good anyway, then the condition will come. In other words, let the emotional response be what you are looking for first. Allow the good feeling of what you want to be the goal.

To say to yourself, "I'll be happy when this occurs" depicts non-alignment with the thing you want. If you think you will be happy at a future moment, what is your reason to delay feeling happiness now? Time does not wait for you, so why would you wait for time?

You simply cannot get what you want from feeling the absence of your desire. The familiar expression, "You can't get there from here," appropriately articulates the dilemma. The origin of this American English phrase is primarily attributed to the people of Maine. Apparently when asked for directions to a place located outside a local vicinity, often the response contained the aforementioned phrase based upon the difficulty of describing a route. Consequently, the problem cannot be solved from where you stand. Although this may sound like advising one to give up, this is nonetheless an excellent example of how the identifiable use of your feelings can solve any problem through better attention and understanding of their intended purpose.

Suppose you want something that you think of as out of reach in your current physical reality. In your imagination you can see yourself with it and likewise enjoy the feelings associated with having it now. However, as you look around the physical space and do not see what you imagine, an inner dialog may start a conversation in your mind with the intention to reconcile the imbalance. In an effort to harmonize and feel better now, you may hear your own words whisper: "I am only dreaming." This, so to speak, "returning to earth," serves to solidify beliefs you may hold about your dream as being unrealistic compared to the physical reality that you determine as fact based upon evidence from your physical senses of taste, touch, hearing, sight and smell.

If you continue to experience similar emotions associated with your inner conversation about the imaginary nature of your dream; that literally causes you to move away from the feeling of having it now and consequently stops you from going forward to receive your desire in physical form. What emotions do you notice after you have talked yourself out of something you want? Moreover, do you still want it?

Make the emotion (feeling) the big deal because it represents connection to all the resources available that you may not yet see. If you demand the condition before you have the unconditional feeling of having your desire now, you cannot bridge the gap of getting there from where you stand. Another often used cliché, "to put the cart before the horse" means the object of your desire stands waiting for something to move it to you. And if you suppose that you must figure out how to move that cart, think again.

Vibration is a word that best describes feelings. Movement is vibration in action. You can feel movement of air, but do you actually see air moving? More accurately, you see the evidence of air movement after the fact. Your thoughts and associated feelings act precisely in the same manner.

You want something because you believe you will feel better when you have it. Conversely, if something feels bad, you think you will feel better in its absence. Do you hear the simplicity of your power to choose? You can deliberately choose to feel good or you can unconsciously choose to feel bad. You can make this choice for yourself. The relationship with your inner self never pushes against you. Basically, you are always right from your perspective.

You are the exclusive commander of your emotions precisely because you have the power to choose what you will focus upon. Whether or not something feels good or bad, you will receive exactly what you choose to feel about most often. You either feel good or not. Like a donut hole, there is nothing in the middle.

Do yourself a favor and take time to notice the way combinations of your feelings become the experiences in your life that show up as both good and bad from your point of view. To illustrate the enormous power you wield to control your life by enhancing awareness of your feelings, engage in the following activity.

EXERCISE:

From where you stand now, would it be easier for you to (1) deposit fifty million dollars into your bank account this afternoon or (2) to find a thought that feels good around the subject of prosperity and enjoy what you would do with the money now?

1. In your response to the question above, are you experiencing sensations of ease, relief, calmness, belief, and an inner awareness of knowing it is done? Or, are you thinking about how, who, where or when? What words would you use to describe your emotions?

    Remember, whatever you are feeling is information you can use now. Your feelings act as a built-in guidance system that operates with absolute precision. Every emotion you encounter entices you to own it and ultimately move upward to an even better sensational feeling.
2. Write down your response and look at it. Read it aloud and notice your feelings.
3. Mental resistance is the act of pushing against something you do not want in hope that it will change or go away. If you have noticed an unpleasant feeling, ask yourself a question: "How much of my energy am I deliberately giving to something I do not want and what am I willing to do about it now?

The attention you give to feeling good as you move through your day is powerful. There is no law of exclusion or redemption. There is no law of repentance and there is likewise no law of undoing. You are not required to relive any experience in hope that it will change the fact that it happened or that it will even cause you to feel better about it now. For if you want to relive and dwell upon something previously done and feel those associated emotions again, remember, you are definitely creating more of the same thing. Often referred to as the definition of insanity—repeating the same action and expecting a different result—is both empowering and hilarious to consider. This is especially empowering when you understand that it is you who makes the actionable choice. Nothing outside of you has the power to create your life experiences because you are the only person occupying your physical body. There is, quite literally, no other person in there but you.

Most importantly, understand that you have zero power to cause another person to change their mind. Everyone does this for themselves regardless of external persuasions offered by other people. It does not matter how strong a message gets delivered or how compelling it may appear. It is always a personal choice to take action irrespective of what you may believe to the contrary. Profoundly, your power of choice is one of your greatest assets readily available and under your absolute control.

Simple does not mean *easy*. "Uncomplicated" may be a better word to explain the meaning of simple. It is the combination of simple things woven together that often makes a thing appear to be complicated. Test this out for yourself by examining one of your more elaborate dreams. Who or what determines the complicated sequences other than the creator of the dream? To see your dream in its entirety provides you with the clear vision of the simplicity to allow it to manifest naturally into your physical reality.

> *"Hold fast to your dreams, for if dreams die, life is a broken-winged bird that cannot fly.*
> *Hold fast to dreams for when dreams go, life is a barren field frozen with snow."*
> —LANGSTON HUGHES

THE NON-CONTRADICTED MIND

One day while out for a walk around a local marina, I decided I would enjoy going for a boat ride. While easy enough to accomplish with the purchase of a ticket, my goal for a ride happened to extend to a private sail aboard a non-commercially owned vessel. I wanted someone to invite me to go sailing. At the time I did not know anyone who would accommodate my request, so it became a dream I decided to expand while walking along the footpath that overlooked a variety of boats docked in the marina.

As far as dreams go, it is usually more fun to dream big. Therefore, turning my attention to the boats that I considered beautiful, I stepped into the feeling of enjoying a smooth ride on the water while seated in a lap of luxury. The fun part in this particular fantasy moved rapidly with the sight of every boat I chose to mentally step aboard.

A part of my regular exercise routine includes walking and listening to my own voice recordings of affirmations, music or other inspirational messages. My earphones also serve as a gentle stop sign to passersby. With my ears filled with the buds emitting joyful sounds, this affords an effortless experience to maintain the imaginative world I choose to bask in during my walks. To physically walk inside of my dream momentarily becomes a very real physical reality with the aid of a set of earphones. Essentially, this is the way I give myself permission to enjoy the feeling of having what I want immediately.

Fresh air and calm surroundings always contribute to the overall pleasure of taking a walk. Even though the familiar scenery appears unchanged, the activity in the scenes constantly changes. Birds, marine life, people and boats passing by are fun to observe. In this coastal area, California sea lions entertain onlookers as they swim throughout the harbor and frequently jump onto the docks and boat transoms. As uninvited guests, sea lions often bulldoze their way past inflatable air dancers and colorful bucket barriers in order to temporarily inhabit a dry space.

As cute and amusing as sea lions look, it is better for them to stick to relaxing on the outer rocks because of an unmissable stench that comes and goes as their numbers increase. I find it entertaining and funny to listen to people speak about how uncaring they may find the harbor patrol officers' efforts to control the behavior of our marine friends. The officers sometimes spray the sea lions with fire-hose-strength water to encourage them to move on. If those onlookers could see from the eyes of a boat owner, they would readily understand the other side of dealing with these wonderful creatures who have no knowledge about bathroom decorum.

As it happens, smell is one sensation tricky to ignore. A sudden unpleasant odor shocked me back on land from my fantasy boat ride musings. Immediately picking up my pace, I walked briskly toward rounding a corner some distance away from a growing pinniped group sunning themselves on a nearby dock. Sea lions are certainly more delightful to observe from a distance beyond which the human nose can detect their scent versus close proximity to their resting places.

Customarily, I will speak to people and offer a smile as our paths cross. Today, a man maneuvering his sail boat into a slip waved and shouted hello to me as I passed by. A little tired from my steady two-and-a-half-mile walk, I decided to stop and watch this man steer his vessel into the narrow slip space. Admiring his smooth and expert landing, I asked him if he had a good time out on the water. He smiled and told me it was delightful. Ready to continue on my way, quite abruptly, the man asked me; "Would you like to go sailing sometime?"

Not more than ten minutes earlier I remembered that I wanted an invitation and I had placed no particular condition upon my request. In fact, I became so involved in my imaginary boat ride that it shocked me to hear a complete stranger ask me the relevant question out loud.

Awareness of the absence of something makes it very difficult to find the path that leads directly to the thing wanted. This happens because of the vibration you stand in—the absence. Observing the opposite of what you want will always cloud your vision. The moment you know what you want, see it and accept that you have been given it immediately. It is yours and it is alive in your imagination. Because you are given your request immediately in the form of a vibration, you must tune into the vibration of what you have asked for so you can translate the vibration into its equivalent physical manifestation.

The most expedient way to receive is to avoid contemplating the absence of what you want and pay close attention to the way you feel. In simpler words, feel and enjoy the end result immediately. Recall to mind the universal order of things and you will begin to understand that a feeling will always come first.

During my fantasy dream of enjoying a ride on a private sail boat, I literally stepped into the feeling of having it now with unconditional love. Specifically, my thoughts pointed directly to things working out the way I wanted them to and I loved every moment of my idea.

Ultimately, the thing you want will come to you. You do not have to concern yourself with "how" because that is beyond your control.

My answer to the man's question flew out of my mouth with words that surprised me as I vocalized my response. "Yes, I would love to go sailing. What about tomorrow? I'll bring lunch. By the way, what is your name?"

Simon and I agreed on a time, exchanged goodbyes and I briskly walked to my car. Along the way I thought about what I would say to my husband. I had just accepted an invitation to go sailing with a man I barely knew. Drifting into a continuation of my earlier fantasy, blissful feelings guided me home as I gave way to the waves of gratitude that effortlessly streamed to and through me. I was absolutely thrilled and grateful to have received an invitation to go sailing.

The choice you make for a spouse may be one of the more important decisions in your life. To share some of your precious time and attention with another person on a regular basis requires understanding yourself in greater detail. Basically, you will give yourself the gift of companionship and there will be a price to pay. As long as you give love, you will reap the rewards of like kind in plentiful ways.

Respect for another person surely ranks at the top of the list in terms of maintaining a good relationship. One of the things I love and enjoy about my husband is his grown-up attitude.

"When I became a man I put away childish things, including the fear of childishness and the desire to be very grown up."—C.S. Lewis

With great joy and enthusiasm, I described to my husband my encounter, the invitation and my intention to go sailing the next day. His words of wisdom still ring in my ears: "Have a good time." He cheerfully delivered his message to me while giving me a hug and a kiss.

Floating on the ocean under the power of wind filling a sail that effortlessly pushes a boat through water remains one of the greater joys of allowing nature to help you have a good time. You can hear the sound of the water as you glide through it with the non-resistant precision of a sharp knife cutting through butter. There is much to learn about wind movement. Zephyr, the ancient Greek god of the west wind, need not trouble your decision to allow the breeze to guide your actions in setting the sail. During the ride with my new friend Simon, I learned about his experience as a captain and becoming a master sailor from earlier adventures in his youth. This man knew more about the wind than anyone I have ever met.

Accompanied by Simon's two dogs who probably knew as much about sailing as their owner, we all enjoyed lunch and sightings of dolphins displaying their ability to jump and swim with the greatest of ease.

Returning to the shore, or to earth depending on your perspective, completed a fun-filled afternoon. As with all experiences, a journey ultimately leads you to an angle of repose as it likewise opens a door for yet another idea to carry you to a new destination. You can absolutely enjoy more good things as you make the conscious decision to do so.

GIVE YOURSELF PERMISSION TO DO WHAT YOU WANT TO DO

Suggestion is a powerful tool. You can use the power of suggestion on other people and also on yourself. Because many people are readily open to listening to stories that do not feel good, it is possible to actively notice one of the ways that stops you from feeling good all of the time.

Shockingly enough, negative stories are often given a great deal of time and attention. To what end will it serve you to give prolonged or marginal attention to anything that does not feel good? If you think that you must look at something you do not want in order to figure out what you do want, that makes sense. Asking repeatedly for something you want and contrasting it with something you do not want, eventually forms a perplexing belief as to your worthiness to receive the desired good thing you rightly deserve.

"By the powerful Universal Law of Attraction, you draw to you the essence of whatever you are predominantly thinking about. If you are predominantly thinking about the things you desire, your life experience reflects those things. And in the same way, if you are predominantly thinking about what you do not want, your life experience reflects those things."—Esther and Jerry Hicks

Inside of you exists a vivacious person that consistently pursues happiness but sometimes may veer in contradictory directions unintentionally. Edna St. Vincent Millay wrote:

> "The world stands out on either side
> No wider than the heart is wide;
> Above the world is stretched the sky,
> No higher than the soul is high.
> The heart can push the sea and land;
> Further away on either hand;
> The soul can split the sky in two,
> And let the face of God shine through.
> But East and West will pinch the heart
> That cannot keep them pushed apart;
> And he whose soul is flat—the sky
> Will cave in on him by and by."

To become a master of anything continues to be an easy thing to do. You have already mastered numerous actions that serve you and others very well. Repeatedly doing things in a certain way is how everyone becomes an expert. You are an expert at being the person you imagine yourself to be.

A dictionary definition of the word "master," used as a noun, describes a person who rules others or has control, authority or power over something. Used as a verb, *to master*, describes the way repeated actions taken up by someone render them excellent in execution of a particular thing. A person who becomes extremely skilled at a particular activity through repetition is therefore considered to be a Master.

You are the master of yourself. And as you sharpen the skills of your particular interests with the intention of getting better at whatever you choose to do, mastery can be claimed and effortlessly expressed through your actions. Choice is your tool to use to master feeling good.

"I am in the pursuit of happiness. Things are always working out for me. I live happily ever after because I am after happiness."—Victoria Winters

part three
AFFIRMATION

chapter seven

ABSOLUTE POWER–APPLY MAGNUM FORCE

"Struggle sucks, adversity is painful and obstacles are irritating. The only thing worse is when none of these things occur. There's something about winning without a fight that's unsatisfying. The victory is embedded in the battle."
—Steve Siebold

Words spoken out loud, from your voice, reenter your mind and tend to align with feelings associated around the idea conveyed. Bluntly, what you say about yourself matters tremendously. It matters because you believe your own words. You are the creator of your own self-image. Irrespective of whether an idea you entertain comes from another person, it is the act of speaking words to yourself over and over again that initiates your beliefs and activates your faith, whether you like the idea or not.

Words are precise combinations of characters which carry a minimum of one meaning that gets saved in one location much like information stored in a computer hard drive. A word is a brief expression, statement, remark, assurance, promise, command or affirmation. Your ability to recall and repeat information serves you in much the same manner as a computer facilitates recall of whatever you ask it to deliver. The difference in your memory power over a machine pales in comparison to the absolute unlimited stream of power flowing to and through you.

Energetic power under your control can be used positively or inverted to a lower purpose. However, it is the outcome of lower application of energy which dilutes the strength to affect the thing you want to bring forth. This is a fancy way of saying that you get what you think about and emotionalize over most often whether it feels good or not. You are magnificent, important, influential, worthy and have direct access to the power that creates worlds.

In all realities there is no such thing as something for nothing. You are the only one who offers yourself a positive or negative vibration by your attention to thoughts inside of your own mind. Life is such a beautiful phenomenon. The things you want are delivered to you based on your vibrational proximity to them because of your feelings and attention paid to your own thought patterns. Subsequently, hard work is not required to achieve anything you really want.

One way to better understand life from an atypical perspective is to realize you were born with everything you need and from that point forward you choose things you want. Essentially, your entire life experiences are based on your own choices. Numerous gifts beyond the basic sustenance of life preservation are initially provided by parents or other persons engaged in raising a human from infancy to adolescence and/or adulthood. To sustain life, humans require food, shelter, clothing and love. Beyond these essential necessities, everything else falls under the category of desire.

What gets in your way is your thoughts about what you think you must do in order to achieve something you want. Fortunately, an abundance of all things is available for your selection. By the power of choice, you can cause the thing you think about to be created and delivered to you effortlessly. Thoughts are things.

Many wise people offer this good advice: Associate with like-minded individuals to manage your energetic power more efficiently. Rightly noted, if you tell another person about your intentions and ask them to hold you accountable, you will most likely do as you say.

An agreement between two or more people to move toward a common goal, (get a personal project done) is a concept older than recorded history. A proverb written in 1546 by John Heywood in the early modern English style of that distant era speaks of a simple concept and practice still in use today. *"Some heades haue taken two headis better then one: But ten heads without wit, I wene as good none."* Although a challenge to read, pronounce and interpret in today's vernacular, you may know this phrase as commonly spoken: *"Two heads are better than one."*

All people wield the potential power to energetically create the objects of their desire. This power perpetually runs to and through you. Your own command allows you to constrict the energy flow of this great power. It is good to know that nothing outside of you can ever diminish or eliminate your ability to utilize this tremendous gift. "Can you or anyone else stop the wind from blowing? The power to choose a thought is always within your control.

MIND THE MASTER—MASTER THE MIND

Accountability partners or mastermind groups are easy to establish. Often articulated; there is power in numbers; to be clear, the number is up to you. A team of two can be just as powerful and effective as a group of ten or more. If you would like to help others, share your project ideas. Be willing to listen to the other person, to ask questions and to allow yourself to respond versus react. A mastermind group requires nothing more than your willingness to connect with another person, maintain an open mind and mutually agree to help each other to focus on good thoughts and ideas during each session. With those priorities at hand, go ahead and start your own group. To give value to another person from a place of observant love, positions you to see the good in another person. Relentless pursuit to spot something good will reveal to you the endless supply of happiness resident inside of you. From your abundance of happiness, you can use this positive energy more effectively. When you give the gift of your attention to the good you see in the other person, together you will rise to your individual great expectations.

As a participant in my own accountability groups, I enjoy the pleasure of interacting with people on subjects of mutual interest. Adopting the concept of one size fits many, it becomes easy to identify and to choose like-minded partners. *One-size fits many* does not mean that everyone is the same size or that they intend to do exactly the same thing. Even if two people are engaged in similar projects, they will perform their tasks in their unique style. Therefore, you can relax and enjoy listening and sharing ideas with other people because the goal is to expand and make manifest good ideas resident in both your mind and the mind of the other person.

To decide to be happy is profoundly the best choice you can undertake in any given moment. The present moment is the only time you can make a choice and it makes sense to first notice how you feel and then choose a thought that feels better.

Overthinking is a habit that prevents you from taking action. When you think too much, instead of acting and doing things, you overthink. Often, you may not be aware when you over analyze, comment and repeat the same thoughts over and over instead of taking action. An accountability partner who actively listens to you can pinpoint the moments when you are engaged in overthinking. Their call for you to "get out of your own way" expressed in a direct and colorful way, (sh*t or get off the pot) may be the very thing you need to catapult yourself into action.

"Thinking was made to order what you want, not to indulge in it. The mind is there to receive the order and make it appear to you. Thinking isn't needed for anything else because everything else is taken care of by Awareness"—RHONDA BYRNE'S, TEACHER

One of my accountability partners occasionally drops word bombs that hit my funny bone and cause me to laugh out loud. I have heard many expletives spoken by people who use them in public settings to indicate their dislike for the status quo. However, my dear friend commands the English language expertly as he speaks with his soft New England accent. And it is highly amusing when he inserts certain unexpected words to convey an idea. For the most part, this way of lightening a potentially heavy conversation serves to make his point more memorable.

Another accountability partner and likewise dear friend, speaks with a Welsh accent that automatically commands one to listen attentively. Some of the words he chooses contain connotations that differ from American English and a bit of translation becomes necessary from time to time. Overall, it is delightful to my ears to hear the sound of his English words enunciated in a style more akin to the origins of the language.

From New England to western Australia and back to California, the three of us are friends and accountability partners who share a common interest in raising our awareness about who we really are. Our weekly meetings endure despite the time zone differences between our world-wide locations. Of particular relevance, we are individually engaged in our unique lifestyles, interests, family compositions and careers. One of the best things about an accountability group is the collective power each individual brings to increase each members' overall well-being. When you work with synergy in the spirit of one for all and all for one, the combined effect is greater than the sum of separate efforts. Consequently, absolute power is at your command.

The present is your point of power. Everything happens in the present moment. You cannot take action in the past or future. The past is recalled by memory and the future is imagined in your marvelous mind. If you assign greater attention to anything in the past and think of it as an energy that has power over you, then you will feel ineffective and deny yourself your real power to create what you really want to enjoy. It is easier to feel good first and allow the conditions of those feelings to follow as they must.

Carefully paying attention to your feelings and asking yourself questions will increase your ability to better control your lifestyle, situations and circumstances. Parents, family members, friends, associates and strangers contribute and, to some extent, continue to offer ideas that you may or may not like or choose to act upon. You choose to select what to allow into your personal thought process. Only you can choose to change anything that no longer serves your purpose. As you become the person you observe in your imagination, you consciously direct your mind to obey your command of the idea you want to project.

Well-being is larger than you may realize. Life flows to and through your physical body. You possess and partake of food, shelter, clothing and love. Life is good. Goodness prevails and always outweighs and overrides bad in all its forms. There is nothing greater than good. Because well-being abounds, it is curious that many people choose to pick one small irritation, focus and concentrate on it until it blinds them to the overall goodness ever present in their own life.

Fortunately, you are the only one who can make yourself happy or sad. By performing a simple exercise, you can give yourself an immediate glimpse of your extraordinary power and learn exactly how to make yourself happy during your waking hours.

EXERCISE

1. Choose something very insignificant that you like and blow it up in the same manner you would give attention to something that annoys you.
2. Speak positive words to describe the thing you choose to embellish. Even if it concerns a cup of coffee, talk about

it as if it were the best drink on earth. Pour emotion into your words until you feel the words activate a sensation within. Above all, do not force anything to happen as you speak. (Note: You can do this in writing if you choose; however, read your written words aloud.)
3. Listen carefully to your words and notice how you feel. Keep going until you recognize the blissful feeling of absolute joy. Then, gently expand your conversation from that point forward. Enjoy the good feeling. Become aware that you use this same approach for everything whether you are paying attention to how you feel or not. It is always your action upon thoughts that cause you to feel a certain way. Even if you think it may be another person who triggers you to react or respond, it is only you who actually directs yourself to react or respond. This is a practice of paying attention to how you feel and doing something about it.

You take yourself with you everywhere you go. And it is especially nice to know that you can feel happy all the time and in any place by choice. The point is, you always use the power of choice. As you deliberately direct your power, decide to enjoy the reactions that return to you effortlessly. Giving attention to what you want that feels good by simply observing the feeling of it will help you to make new choices that align with feeling good. It is this action that elevates your mood and aligns you with similar vibrations. Like attracts like and it doesn't matter if it feels good or bad, but it definitely matters which feeling dominates. You can do this because you are the supreme master and commander of your marvelous mind.

"Watch what thou seeth, and lightly bring me word." —ALFRED, LORD TENNYSON

LET VARIETY KEEP JOY AND BALANCE IN YOUR LIFE

*"As long as habit and routine dictate the pattern of living, new dimensions of the soul will not emerge.—*Henry Van Dyke

Routine, a sequence of actions regularly followed, can make you lazy or at the very least bored with your life. On the other hand, a set of customary and often mechanically performed procedures or activities often work to your advantage. Preparing for the day, most people incorporate fairly mechanical patterns to accomplish grooming and dressing. More often than not, some people have too many routines that trap them in sameness and ultimately impede growth and expansion of new and perhaps more exciting life experiences. What to do about it becomes the question that often gets answered by simply doing more of the same old things.

If you would like to do something different, you can do so by changing some routines. Flexibility will help you bend in new directions without breaking your most ardent sequences which contribute to your overall feelings of well-being. You may have heard people say that you need to go beyond your comfort zone to set yourself free. Well, if going beyond your comfort zone makes you nervous, you will most likely avoid taking that step. However, there are other ways to heed that advice without hanging yourself out to dry.

A list is a useful tool. In fact, you can make a list easily. The commonly known "To Do" list works for many people, but it also fails many because of lack of use. One of my accountability partners suggests renaming the proverbial list to "Things I Want To Do." Although he does not claim credit for the original idea, it offers a different point of view from which to approach a previously envisioned idea.

TWELVE WAYS TO CHANGE YOUR ROUTINES

1. Read different subjects—astronomy, art, physics, music, photography.
2. Change your routes to places you often go.
3. Make new friends and/or hang out with different people.
4. Do your work somewhere new or take breaks from coworkers.
5. Differ the times you do things.
6. Reorganize a closet or drawer—make room for something new.
7. Create new eating habits or change your eating schedule.
8. Turn off the television—read a book, relax, take a walk, listen to music, play a game.
9. Play a musical instrument or learn to play one.
10. Learn a new language—tell a story to someone in your new language.
11. Take a trip—go somewhere near-by or book a one-night stay in a new location and stay five days.
12. Be flexible—decide to make your life more exciting and interesting to you.

Affirm to yourself that things are always working out for you. Actually, everything works out for you because you live to tell the stories of your previous experiences. Have you given yourself credit for conquering the obstacles that did not stop you from landing in your present place?

Let a good feeling be the prize you are looking for. It is the emotional good feeling of the thing you want that really rings your bell. Feeling always precedes physical manifestation.

A favorite near-by destination is one of the California Channel Islands. Santa Catalina, located off the coast of southern California, is a popular destination for day trips and weekend getaways. Hosting a full-time resident population of approximately four-thousand people, the residents live primarily in the island's only incorporated city, Avalon. The island is twenty-two miles long and eight miles across at its widest. The rocky hills topography serve as home to a variety of birds, small mammals and even American bison, who roam freely throughout interior grassy valleys. In 1924 fourteen bison were brought to the island to film a western motion picture. However, the scenes containing the bison landed on the cutting room floor and never made it to the big screen. Due to cost overruns the film company decided to leave the bison on the island. The size of the bison herd today is maintained at approximately one-hundred-fifty strong.

"To the island-valley of Avilion; Where falls not hail, or rain, or any snow, nor ever wind blows loudly; but it lies deep-meadow'd, happy, fair with orchard lawns and bowery hollows crown'd with summer sea, where I will heal me of my grievous wound."—IDYLLS OF THE KING BY ALFRED, LORD TENNYSON, WRITTEN BETWEEN 1859–1885.

Catalina has a warm-summer Mediterranean climate and very mild winters. The average temperatures in January range between 58°F to 48°F and July temperatures average from approximately 60°F to 78°F. Measurable rainfall averages 45 days a year and there is rarely snowfall on the island.

People have inhabited the island for over seven thousand years. European explorer Juan Rodriguez Cabrillo first named the island San Salvador after his sailing ship. Claimed for his country Spain, sixty years later, (1602) explorer Paulo Coelho (1548–1624) reclaimed the island and renamed it in honor of St. Catherine's Feast Day, (November 24) in the year 1602. Catherine of Alexandria, also known as Saint Catherine of Alexandria (c.286–305), according to legend, was the daughter of Constus, (c. 206–306) the governor of Alexandria during the reign of roman emperor Maximian Herculius (250–310). Indeed, it is fascinating to observe the way stories of unknown truth tend to live on and influence decisions in a present moment.

During the times I visit Catalina, I make it a point to learn something new and to engage in at least one out-of-my-ordinary activity. The word "history" contains two words, "his" and "story." I find it amusing that Spanish explorers Juan Rodriguez Cabrillo and Paulo Coelho both claimed and named the same island. It is fascinating to recognize how a point of view presented by one or more people reveals that opportunities are everywhere and especially right in front of you.

At the point of noticing anything you do not like, it is easy to see its opposite. Irrespective of past actions by you or others, it not only feels better to think about what you want, but it is easier to take action toward creating it. Your beliefs are thoughts that you can and should question.

You are going to do things throughout the days and years of your life. The contrast of circumstances, situations and acquisition of things you may both like and dislike helps you to discover new ways to enjoy every experience of your life. Spend a little more time every day imagining what you want to experience and remember your personal successes. When you feel enthusiasm to do something, it means you have lined up the energy and are being inspired to take action from that point of alignment. From there, go forward and watch what happens.

Abraham Hicks says: "You are the creator of your own experience. You must create your experience deliberately to have the joyful experience you are meant to have. Unless you are seeing the world through the eyes of source, then you are but a shadow of the being you have come forth to be. If you are doing less than loving whatever you are giving your attention to, you are not who you were really born to be."

Living life on your terms is the absolute power you get to use by the application of choosing what you want from the sheer love of feeling good.

"When you care about how someone else feels about you, then you do them a disservice. Come into alignment with goodness by caring about what you think of yourself. Raising your vibrational state of being projects pure positive energy to others."—Victoria Winters

chapter eight

ONE QUESTION A DAY— AN AFFIRMATION IN PLAY

Day 1

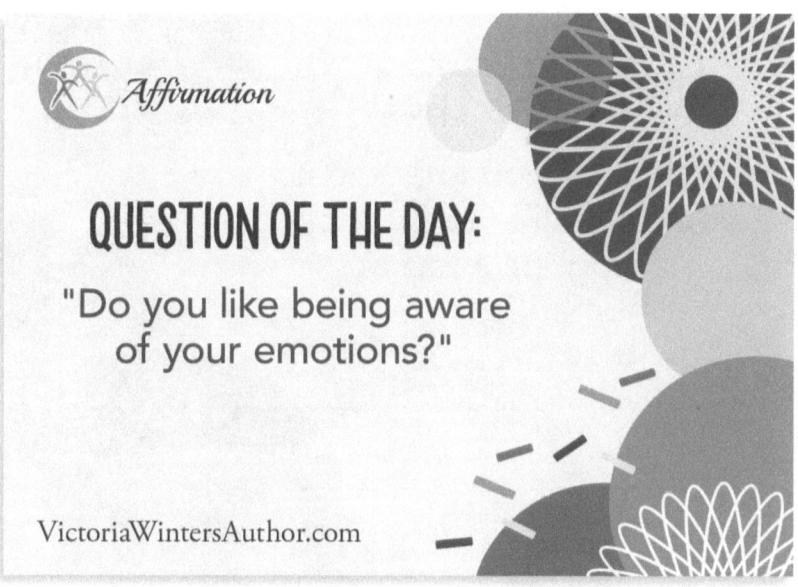

"I am so happy and grateful now that I am in control of the thoughts I choose to increase my awareness about my perpetual well-being."

Day 2

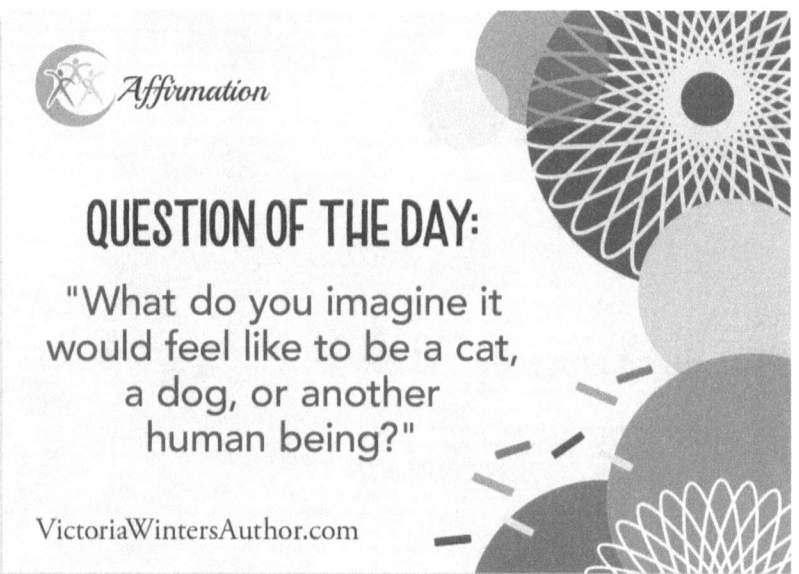

*"I am so happy and grateful now that
I have every reason to expect positive expectations."*

Day 3

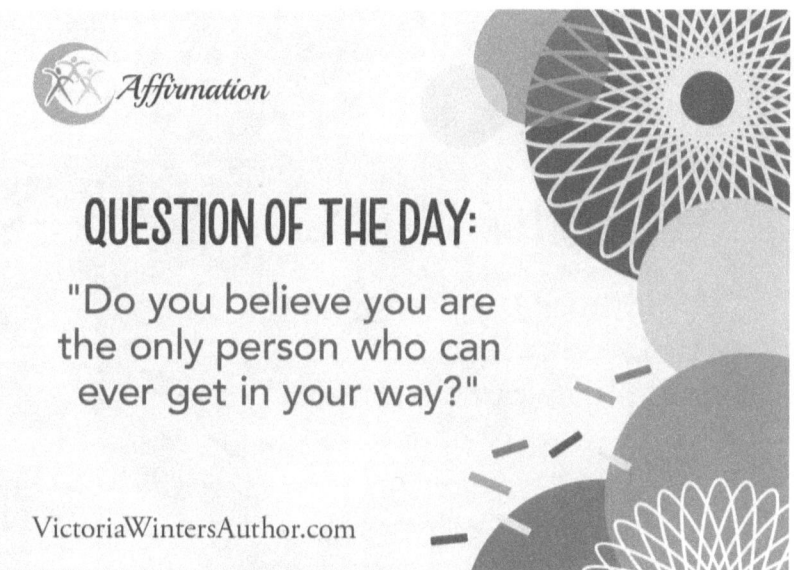

*"I am so happy and grateful now that
I remember life is supposed to be fun."*

Day 4

"I am so happy and grateful now that everything always works out for me."

Day 5

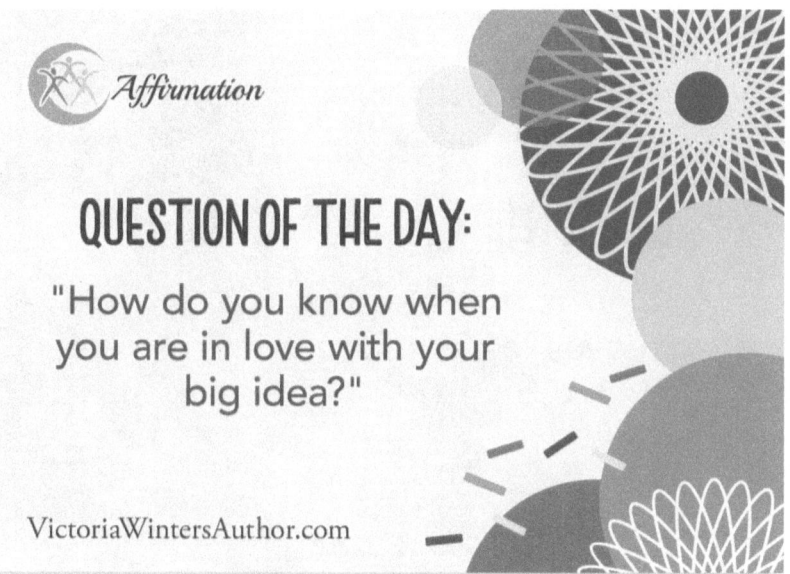

*"I am so happy and grateful now that
I love the life I create for myself."*

Day 6

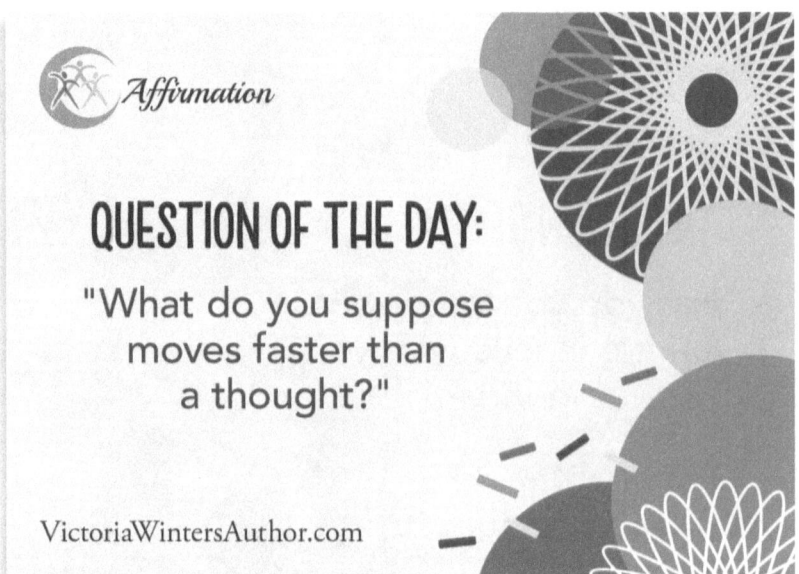

*"I am so happy and grateful now that
I know my goals are worthy of me."*

Day 7

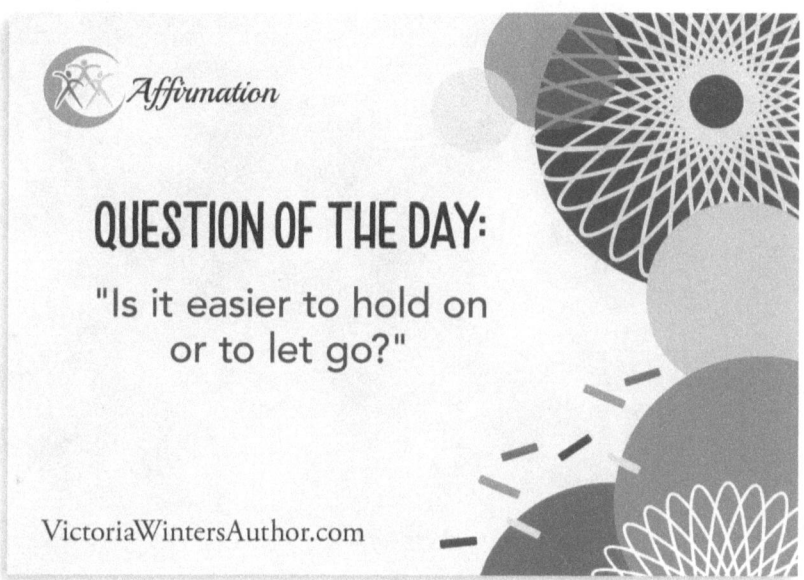

"I am so happy and grateful now that no other person must do anything in order for me to feel good."
Awareness precedes choice.

Expand your awareness—See more!

chapter nine

GOOD—THE ONLY REALITY OF BEING

*"Life is a perpetual doing, not a perpetual wrestling.
No one can grow for us, and it all depends upon ourselves
how rapidly and how strongly we shall grow."*
—Thomas Troward

G RATITUDE PLACES YOU on the path of all good that you want and already possess. Sandy Gallagher, Proctor Gallagher Institute, says: *"It's not who we are that holds us back, it's who we think we are not."* Everyone is creative, yet no one has ever seen the mind; however, everyone experiences activities of mind. Mind is movement, not a thing. In order to gain clarity of purpose, see the pictures of what you desire. There is a better way to do whatever you are doing, and it is up to you to do the things you want and love in your own way. The more you understand what you are doing while feeling grateful that you can do whatever you want, the better control you gain over yourself and ultimately your results.

Every person wants to feel alive and goes about their way of validating existence. If you were to replace the words *right* and *wrong* with working or not working, this may enlarge your perspective about your worthiness of all the good surrounding you in life.

"When we love, we always strive to become better than we are. When we strive to become better than we are, everything around us becomes better too."—Paulo Coelho de Souza

Trusting yourself is an integral practice you can improve through questioning your beliefs and paying greater attention to the way you feel. You do not necessarily rise to the level of your expectations because your practices are the level on which you fall. There is a decided difference between something working or not working as opposed to it being right or wrong.

When the value judgment of "right or wrong" is placed upon one of your actions, it can feel as if a trap door opens, grabs you and drags you to a place of uncertain trust in yourself. That trap is your belief in an idea that there is a "right" or "wrong" way to do something. Whose ideas are you adhering to when you deem one of your actions as right or wrong? Would it not feel better and heighten trust in yourself to ponder whether something is working or not working?

You lead yourself and increase awareness as you explore the possibilities of doing things in certain and new ways. The nineteenth century writer, Wallace Wattles, expresses the idea of trust in yourself with encouraging and repetitive statements in his book titled *The Science of Getting Rich*.

> *"There is a thinking stuff from which all things are made, and which, in its original state, permeates, penetrates, and fills the interspaces of the universe.*
>
> *A thought, in this substance, produces the thing that is imaged by the thought.*
>
> *Man can form things in his thought, and, by impressing his thought upon formless substance, can cause the thing he thinks about to be created.*
>
> *In order to do this, man must pass from the competitive to the creative mind; he must form a clear mental picture of the things he wants, and do, with faith and purpose, all that can be done each day, doing each separate thing in an efficient manner."*

In Wattles' statements you will not find the words "right" or "wrong" emphasized for use as a tool to determine the effectiveness of what you choose. Therefore, it makes sense to practice trusting yourself more. Let go of being "right" or "wrong" and explore the delightful process of choosing something that works for you. You will feel better every time you make a choice because you will act in the capacity as the real leader of your own life.

Leadership causes movement in your experiences. You lead yourself to follow another person's ideas in the same way you take yourself wherever you wish to go by the thoughts you allow to dominate your vision. Choice is freedom and it is the awareness of your choices that sets you free.

The better you feel, the more open you become to living the dreams you see as desires for greater happiness. You never get life wrong; rather you may find yourself living up to an arbitrary standard of what an outcome should be and how it should be attained. In essence, you allow yourself to believe in things that are not true for you.

Turn your attention toward the excellence you see in your dreams. This will ignite a fire within your incredible mind. Stoke the fire of your passions with affirmative words that declare your worthiness of everything you desire. It is this inner movement of thoughts joined with the expectancy of your desire that causes you to take harmonious action. This is the point where you experience pure, positive pleasure in doing things in a certain way, your way.

GET INTO THE SPIRIT OF ATTRACTION

"There is a mechanical attitude of mind which judges everything by the limitation of past experiences, allowing nothing for the fact that those experiences were, for the most part, results of our ignorance of spiritual law."—THOMAS TROWARD

Today, casual conversations about law of attraction are spoken about more openly than ever before. Rhonda Byrne's book, *The Secret* re-introduced the concept that you can attract anything you want and cause it to come to you by using your imagination. For many people, this sounds like pie in the sky. However, understanding the Law of Attraction and willful adherence in your applications upon things under Law is the reason you can naturally cause things you think about to effortlessly come to you.

I have often heard people say an immediate fortune would be earned if "attraction" could be bottled and made available for sale. Love potions, match makers, numerous books and other manufactured devices designed to attract the opposite sex or a potential mate continuously sell on the open market. Everyone knows there is something about attraction that feels mysterious and often elusive. When you hear a truth, you know it because it resonates with your spirit.

Awareness of vibration is the way every person enters into the spirit of attracting something they want. Your feelings broadcast an invisible signal which attracts a like vibration akin to a magnet invisibly drawing metal objects to it. You can watch things come to you by noticing the intensity of your feelings in any given moment. The good feelings about the images you see in imagination start its movement toward you.

By the words, "think into form," you can feel the means of creating anything you have in mind. For where else would you find something to create and bring forth?

The manifestations that appear to you in physical form are a direct result of attraction and your willingness to enter into the spirit of love for your desire. Napoleon Bonaparte boldly affirmed: *"I see only the objective; the obstacle must give way."* This attitude of mind is where your power to live life on your terms resides. You've got the power now to become the person you want to be.

You "feel" because of intuition or tuning to a specific frequency or vibration. Imagination is your workshop of creative endeavors. It is your choice of thoughts to place before yourself in which to interact and blend together into ideas that become your objects of desire. The movement of any idea is directed by your will or focus. As attention to your idea enlarges, the intensity of attractiveness expands and draws everything necessary for the fulfillment of your dream.

Using your will infuses livingness to your new desire. As if by magic you will see things happening before your physical eyes. You will feel the vibrations of your objective subtly moving into form while you proceed.

As you look at your creations in imagination, use your perception to see multiple views from different vantage points. The vibration of one thought broadcasts on a single vibratory level. Notice all the different levels of energy movement within an idea and where they connect in your conscious awareness. Introduce more thoughts that feel good to you, that are in harmony and work intricately with your original idea. Allow nothing to the contrary to pass through the gate guarding entrance to your creative workshop.

Let go of anything that feels out of sync with your intention. Use your memory to recall each component of your idea for a thorough examination. Willingness to read, write, see, hear, taste, touch, smell and move your head and limbs are all choices you make for yourself. From time to time, pause, look at what you are doing and ask a question. "Is what I am doing now working for me and taking me in the direction that feels better?"

The vision of what you want and see in imagination lives on a frequency high above things that appear tangible on the physical plane. Imagination requires your specific focus and must not be compared to anything. This entirely new object of your desire deserves a chance to live. Only you can ensure its life, so give love to nurture and care for it as it grows. Understand that it only takes a bit of poison to kill and that poison is a negative thought.

Deliberately think thoughts that lead you in the direction of your desires. Remember your successes and regularly bring to mind only those successes. That feels good and that is always what you want—to feel good. You are absolutely marvelous!

"Master your choice to feel good."

APPENDIX

SOURCES

Brickhouse, Thomas C., and Smith, Nicholas D. Plato's Socrates. United Kingdom, Oxford University Press, 1994.

Kipling, Rudyard, Rewards and Fairies. Double Day, Page, & Company, 1910.

Holliwell, Raymond, Working With The Law. Revised edition, Life-Success Productions LLC, 2007.

Troward, Thomas, The Hidden Power. Robert M. McBride & Company, 1922.

Hill, Napoleon, Think and Grow Rich. First Jeremy P. Tarcher/Penguin delux edition, 2008.

Allen, James, As A Man Thinketh. First Jeremy P. Tarcher/Penguin Group, 2009

Heywood, John, The Proverbs and Epigrams of John Heywood (A.D. 1562). Reprinted from the original (1562) edition, Printed for the Spenser Society (by Charles Simms and Co.), from Book of Collections of Harvard University, 1867.

Byrne, Rhonda, The Greatest Secret. Harper Collins, 2020.

Wattles, Wallace, The Science of Getting Rich. Proctor Gallagher Institute, 2014.

RECOMMENDED READING

This abbreviated list of recommended books, in the category of Self-Help/Personal-Development, may bring you inspiration, extraordinary value and motivation. The author's original copyright date is included for reference. Enjoy!

> *"The best thing you can do for the world is to make the most of yourself."*

The Power of Awareness by Neville—© 1952
You Were Born Rich by Bob Proctor—© 1984
Think and Grow Rich by Napoleon Hill—© 1937
Ask and It is Given by Esther and Jerry Hicks—© 2004
The Secret by Rhonda Byrne—© 2006
The Science of Getting Rich by Wallace Wattles—© 1910
Awakened Imagination by Neville—© 1954
Your Invisible Power by Genevieve Behrend—© 1921
What to Say When You Talk To Yourself by Shad Helmstetter—© 1982
Your Destiny Switch by Peggy McColl—© 2007
As a Man Thinketh by James Allen—©1903
The Hidden Power by Thomas Troward—© 1921
Working With The Law by Raymond Holliwell—© 1964
You Can Heal Your Life by Louise Hay—©1984
The Power of Now by Echart Tolle—© 1999
Psycho-Cybernetics by Maxwell Maltz—© 1960
A Course In Miracles by Foundation For Inner Peace—© 1975
The Nature of Personal Reality by Jane Roberts—© 1974
The Greatest Salesman in the World by Og Mandino—© 1968
The Power of Your Subconscious Mind by Joseph Murphy—© 1963

ACKNOWLEDGEMENTS

Thank you are two words that embody gratitude. It is with abiding love that I choose to express my appreciation for the people who generously shared their precious time, expertise and support in the writing of this book.

For my family, whom I love unconditionally, I appreciate each of you and especially the individual, unique gifts that you offer to the world and share among family members.

For Dennis, my husband, love of my life, and the grown-up man I adore. Thank you for everything you do to make our marriage an absolute delight. I am a happy wife and I love our life together. I greatly appreciate your "red" pen, insightful spirit and romantic attention to the details of our relationship.

For Crystal, my daughter and friend. You are the woman who holds a precious place in my heart. I feel knowing you all of your life is an honor that shines like the brightest stars in our heavenly universe.

For Evelyn, my mother, thank you for sharing your wisdom, for listening to me and above all, thank you for your kind words of encouragement. I am so happy and grateful that you have been telling me throughout my life to do what I want to do. I am so very fortunate to have you in my life. With love and appreciation to an elegant, beautiful, successful doctor and powerful woman in her own right.

For Kauty, my sister, you are the best. Your creative style and ingenuity consistently uplift and keep the women in our family stylish, radiant and ready for more of the best.

For Arthur, my brother—you are a man with a plan. You've become an outstanding businessman and terrific father. I adore your sense of humor and the entertaining stories you share that keep me smiling and keep our family on the edge of our seats awaiting your next brilliant idea.

For Peggy McColl, my friend and mentor. You are a woman after my own heart. I'm overflowing with gratitude for you and all you do. Thank you for helping me to get out of my own way and write this book. Your encouraging words ring in my ears and I send them back to you; "Your success is absolutely guaranteed." And yes, I am having fun with it!

For Sabrina Norman, my dear friend. Our lives run parallel with many dreams and aspirations we share as businesswomen on a mission of joy. You are inspiring, encouraging, a great story teller, author, and my best friend. Thank you for walking this incredible journey with me.

For Justin Ham, my friend and accountability partner, who lives an ocean's distance away in a southern hemisphere, a land of sunshine. Thank you for lending me an extra pair of eyes. It is a special delight to receive the good vibrations, noteworthy comments, and encouraging words from your peaceful voice.

For Theron Simons, my friend and accountability partner, whose voice beams across the continental United States with a commanding presence that feels like a big hug. Thank you for your strength, gentleness and ever ready animating words that always bring a smile to my face.

*"Go confidently in the direction of your dreams.
Live the life you have imagined."*
—DAVID HENRY THOREAU

RESOURCES

POSITIVE WORDS MATTER

To download, visit:
VictoriaWintersAuthor.com

INCREASE YOUR AWARENESS, USE A GOAL CARD

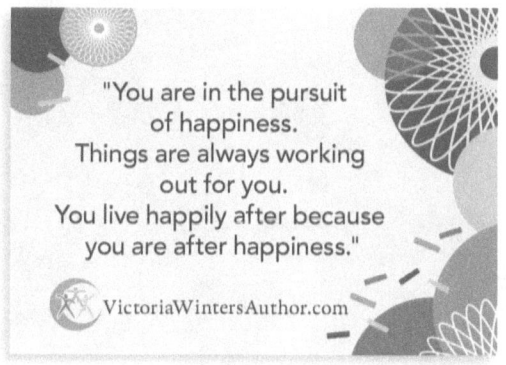

Write your goal in present tense. Feel as if it is yours now as you write. Read it aloud. Carry it with you and read it multiple times a day.

To download, visit:
VictoriaWintersAuthor.com

ABOUT THE AUTHOR

Victoria Winters, known as Ms. Prosperity, is a writer, mentor and entrepreneur in the personal development industry. She specializes in helping people to discover their powerful innate ability to create a lifestyle of excellence, abundant prosperity and absolute happiness. Her tips, tools and mentoring services inspire, uplift and facilitate increasing awareness of the marvelous mind and mental faculties resident within every human being.

As a California native who enjoys sailing, exploring different activities, Victoria also serves on the board of Dana Point Boaters Association, and is lovingly devoted to her husband and family.

Victoria says: "I recognize and feel the enormous power emanating from every human being that is my pleasure to encounter. Your real work is to make the most of yourself. Master the choice to feel good in every moment."

If you are interested in learning more about Victoria's author mentor services visit:
www.VictoriaWintersAuthor.com

www.ingramcontent.com/pod-product-compliance
Lightning Source LLC
Chambersburg PA
CBHW022017290426
44109CB00015B/1209